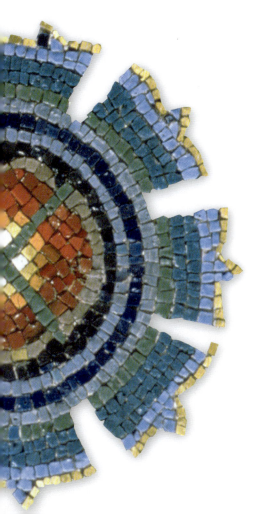

Ravenna
Eight Monuments
World Heritage

Inscription of Ravenna in the Unesco World Heritage List

Texts by Clementina Rizzardi

UNITED NATIONS EDUCATIONAL,
SCIENTIFIC AND
CULTURAL ORGANIZATION

CONVENTION CONCERNING
THE PROTECTION OF THE WORLD
CULTURAL AND NATURAL
HERITAGE

*The World Heritage Committee
has inscribed*

the Early Christian Monuments of Ravenna

on the World Heritage List

*Inscription on this List confirms the exceptional
and universal value of a cultural or
natural site which requires protection for the benefit
of all humanity*

DATE OF INSCRIPTION

7 December 1996

DIRECTOR-GENERAL
OF UNESCO

to Pier Paolo D'Attorre

"The early Christian and Byzantine monuments of Ravenna are of immense importance for the supreme mastery of their mosaic art. Furthermore they represent the proof of artistic and religious connections and contact in an important period of European culture."

It is for this reason that in December 1996 Unesco ratified the inscription of the early Christian monuments of Ravenna in the World Heritage List.

San Vitale, Galla Placidia, the Arian Baptistery and Neonian (Orthodox) Baptistery, Sant'Apollinare Nuovo, Sant'Apollinare in Classe, the Archiepiscopal Chapel, the Mausoleum of Galla Placidia and Theodoric's Mausoleum are now not only the heritage of our city but also of the entire world.

The magnificent early Christian and Byzantine mosaics replete with messages and symbols, the new styles of architecture that blend harmoniously eastern and western influences, the massive structure of the mausoleum dedicated to the King of the Ostrogoths which combines in an unusual way the styles of the different artistic cultures and traditions that have passed through the various periods of Ravenna as capital all represent the distinctive marks thanks to which Unesco has conferred universal acknowledgement of their highly valued uniqueness.

It is a recognition that fills us with pride.

This book, entirely dedicated to what can be considered the "showcase" of our city to the world, brings together the texts of the candidature which enabled Ravenna to be inscribed in the World Heritage List. It describes the beauty of the eight monuments, recounting their history, explaining the reasons for their uniqueness and finally it is intended to document the object of our pride.

There is also another aspect for which we are rightfully proud.

We achieved this objective following, what has become for us, the main line of action in which we have worked in close collaboration with a number of bodies, institutions and private parties in order to reach important goals for the city.

And so it was also for this book. This volume therefore tells another story, the story of close cooperation of the Municipal Administration, the Superintendency, the Archdiocese and the University which in this case has also borne fruit.

We believed in this project and more importantly we believed together and our efforts have been rewarded.

Fabrizio Matteucci
Mayor of Ravenna

There was a time when Ravenna was the capital.

The eight early Christian monuments of Ravenna, recognised by Unesco as World Heritage testify to the greatness of our city in those times.

Furthermore, those monuments tell the story of the Church at the centre of the history of the community; they have passed down to us an extraordinary wealth of religious and spiritual values.

History, art, culture and most of all, faith.

The Church has conserved this gift, maintaining intact their beauty and the religious purpose for which they were built.

Still today the Church of Ravenna feels a strong compulsion to open these places of the "infinite" to the greatest number of people, maintaining their splendour and valorising the perennial transcendental call that emanates from them.

The mosaics are a harmony of mosaic tiles but each tile is indispensable in its originality and independence.

The truth of the Creator's love lives in the free response of every single creature.

In preserving these places the Church of Ravenna cooperates in nourishing all the visitors with the powerful breath of the Spirit which is breather in them.

Monsignor Giuseppe Verucchi
Archbishop of Ravenna - Cervia

The inscription of a site in the World Heritage List by Unesco represents an acknowledgement of the exceptional and unique nature attributed to the eight early Christian and Byzantine monuments in 1996. The city of Ravenna, which is responsible for the site, and the bodies responsible for individual buildings have always understood the inscription in the list not so much as an honorary title simply of decorative value but rather as a precise undertaking to conserve and correctly manage the site as formally requested by Unesco and from which the recognition of the great task entrusted to them arises.

A specially formed work team regularly examines the matters concerning in particular the promotion of knowledge, the exploitation and valorisation of these valuable places considered as a single cultural complex. In this context Law 77/2006 gave the official go-ahead to request financing, a law through which the Ministry of Cultural Heritage and Activities gives economic incentives for the drafting of the management plans requested by Unesco. It is in this context that the new edition of this volume, which brings together the texts presenting the Eight World Heritage Monuments of Ravenna, has been published.

Between 1995 and 1999 in Emilia-Romagna 4 prestigious recognitions were obtained acknowledging the excellence of the region's cultural heritage. In fact over a period of five years UNESCO has inscribed in the World Heritage List the sites of Ferrara – Renaissance City (1995) and its Po Delta (1999), the Early Christian Monuments of Ravenna (1996) and Modena: Cathedral, Civic Tower and 'Piazza Grande' (1997). A regional network of sites of great importance has been created, although consisting of different types (cultural historic town centre and landscape, historic buildings, individual historic building), dating from different periods (late antiquity and Byzantine, medieval, renaissance), having as a common factor the universal value of the sites.

The Regional Administration for Cultural Heritage and Landscape of Emilia-Romagna, together with the Superintendency working in the ambit of the institutional activities of the Ministry of Cultural Heritage and Activities has been involved in the management of three sites and, after cooperating in the drafting of the Management Plans, it now has the objective of unifying the excellent heritage of the three sites in the region under a single plan for their protection, conservation, valorisation and cultural development. This new plan must integrate well with local, national and universal interests and must find the resources necessary for overcoming any obstacles encountered in the variety of subjects involved, the diversity of needs in the field and in the strong sense of identity and intellectual character of the territory.

It is only with the cooperation of all the subjects involved in the management of UNESCO sites that serious valorisation projects can be produced that are capable of creating a valid integrated system for the conservation and promotion of the extraordinary heritage of which we know we are temporary custodians.

Carla Di Francesco
Regional Director for Cultural Heritage and Landscape of Emilia-Romagna

The inscription of the early Christian and Byzantine monuments of Ravenna in the UNESCO World Heritage List is the result of the acknowledgement of their exceptional universal value, their authenticity and integrity.

One century earlier, in 1897, the first superintendency was created in Italy and the priority commitment of the first superintendent, Corrado Ricci, was in fact the restoration of the mosaics and monumental buildings of Ravenna.

The creation of correct methodological and operative practice made it possible to do the restoration work that ensured the protection of the characteristics of authenticity and integrity of the works of art. Thus it was during those years that theoretical knowledge, methods and techniques that form the basis of the practice of architects, art historians and restorers of the Superintendency were formed and which would be used in the delicate and strategic matter of conservation.

The inscription in the World Heritage List is therefore also an acknowledgement of the work done in past years, that constant protection which is obtained through the conservation of an asset. Without conservation valorisation is impossible!

In addition to the valuable skills and abilities acquired in restoration technique, and more generally in the activities of protection and conservation undertaken by the Superintendency, there must also be adequate systems for the management and promotion of cultural assets. The development of these activities must therefore recognise the exceptional universal value, which is the reason for recognition by UNESCO, as the indispensable basis for all measures taken in the territory in regard to the asset.

On the basis of this conviction, the Management Plan of the UNESCO site of Ravenna produced in a highly fruitful collaborative effort by the Municipality, Archdiocese, Superintendency and Regional Administration, is intended as a reference instrument to guide development strategies for the correct and sustainable management of cultural heritage.

The activities of protection and conservation become increasingly indispensable together with the valorisation, promotion and fruition of cultural assets. For this reason there is ever growing interest in the possibility of increasing the effective cooperation of the various bodies involved, each with its own consolidated experience, proven abilities and institutional jurisdiction, and also with thought being given to the possibility of Ravenna's candidature as a European Capital of Culture.

Giorgio Cozzolino
Superintendent for Architectural Heritage and Landscape for the provinces of Ravenna, Ferrara, Forlì-Cesena and Rimini

Index

Prefaces by
Fabrizio Matteucci Mayor of Ravenna — 5
Mons. Giuseppe Verucchi — 7
Carla Di Francesco — 9
Giorgio Cozzolino — 11

Map of the monuments — 14-15

The Mausoleum of Galla Placidia — 16
Historical background — 17
Description — 18
Justification for inclusion in the World Heritage List — 21

The Neonian (Orthodox) Baptistery — 26
Historical background — 27
Description — 28
Justification for inclusion in the World Heritage List — 31

The Arian Baptistery pag. — 34
Historical background — 35
Description — 36
Justification for inclusion in the World Heritage List — 38

The Basilica of Sant'Apollinare Nuovo ag. — 40
Historical background — 41
Description — 42
Justification for inclusion in the World Heritage List — 46

The Archiepiscopal Chapel (Saint Andrew's Chapel) — 50
Historical background — 51
Description — 52
Justification for inclusion in the World Heritage List — 54

Theodoric's Mausoleum — 56
Historical background — 57
Description — 58
Justification for inclusion in the World Heritage List — 60

The Basilica of San Vitale — 64
Historical background — 65
Description — 67
Justification for inclusion in the World Heritage List — 72

The Basilica of Sant'Apollinare in Classe pag. — 78
Historical background — 79
Description — 80
Justification for inclusion in the World Heritage List — 84

Essential Bibliography pag. — 86
Ten years later pag. — 90

5TH CENTURY

Mausoleum of Galla Placidia

Historical Background

The small mortuary chapel situated near to the Basilica of San Vitale and known as the Mausoleum of Galla Placidia was originally connected to the southern side of the narthex of the cruciform Church of Santa Croce which the empress commissioned in the second quarter of the fifth century. According to a fourteenth century source (the *tractatus* by San Rinaldo di Concorreggio) the sacellum was built by Galla Placidia as her own mausoleum however it was not to be used for this purpose as the empress died in Rome in 450 and she was probably buried there in the family mausoleum of Theodosius.

It is generally affirmed that the mausoleum was originally dedicated to Saint Lawrence, who is depicted in mosaic in the lunette facing the door but according to the oldest historical sources (9th century) the sacellum was dedicated to Saint Nazarus.

The present marble floor dates from restoration work done in the 16th century (1540). In 1602 the sacellum was detached from the narthex of S. Croce and thus isolated from its original setting. At that time the original rudimentary door was replaced with a new smaller door at the end of the west side. This door was then closed in 1774 and the original reopened.

Between 1898 and 1902 the building was lined with yellow Siena marble and the previously removed Roman frieze was replaced in its original position above the entrance door.

In 1908 the present day alabaster panels, a gift from King Victor Emanuel III, were installed.

Description

The exterior of the building has a very simple and modest appearance. Built on the plan of a Latin cross (12.75 x 10.25 m) the walls are of coarse short brickwork in layers separated by 2 cm of lime, a traditional constructional feature in the architecture of all of northern Italy.

A brickwork cupola rises where the branches of the building meet, protected by a small quadrangle tower.

Due to subsidence the building cannot be seen in its original proportions as the original floor is about 1.5 m below the present floor level.

With the exception of the façade, once faced with marble panels and connected to the narthex of S. Croce, all the sides of the building are dressed with pilaster strips which embellish and at the same time lighten the external appearance. At the top the pilasters join in a series of high arches and at the bottom they rest on brick plinths which are no longer visible due to the subsidence mentioned previously.

The end of each arm of the building is concluded at the top with a triangular gable within a brick cornice containing a small window. On each side of the drum there is a larger rectangular window while in the lower wall the windows are like narrow slits with embrasures.

The interior of the mausoleum is richly decorated with marble slabs lining the lower walls and mosaics entirely covering the walls, arches, lunettes and cupola in the upper parts. In the cupola an indigo blue sky is illuminated by concentric circles of golden stars which decrease in size towards the centre to give an impression of depth. At the centre a golden Latin cross stands out with its longest arm pointing east and not along the axis of the building which for practical reasons could not be built with this orientation and be connected at the same time to the narthex of S. Croce. The apocalyptic cross is also linked with the symbolic concept of Christ as the rising sun.

The four living creatures of the Apocalypse in connection with the cross are depicted in the pendentives as a lion, a calf, a man and, an eagle, as described in the Revelation of St. John, praising God eternally without ceasing. All four figures depicted in golden mosaic emerge from a bank of stylised multicoloured clouds.

The eschatological cross is also acclaimed by the apostles located in the lower large lunette and represented standing with an arm raised on a blue background merging into yellowish-green lower down, one on each side of the window beneath a broad pavilion in the form of a shell which represents their holiness. The apostles Peter and Paul can be recognised in the lunette on the west side from their typical iconological features. Saint Paul, with pointed beard and balding at the front, is holding a scroll in his left hand while Saint Peter holds the keys of the kingdom of heaven.

The area between each pair of apostles is filled with elegant decorative motifs of symbolic importance: doves facing a *cantharus* from which they drink water or perched on the edge, to symbolise the souls of the saved who quench their thirst at the fountain of divine grace.

Mausoleum of Galla Placidia

Similar concepts are also expressed in the lunettes on the east and west sides at the ends of the transept of the sacellum in which two elegant harts on a background of acanthus leaves drink from a pool illustrating psalm 42 which reads "As the hart panteth after the water brooks, so my soul panteth after Thee, O God".

In the vaults above, Christ's monogram is set within a laurel garland on a background of interweaving vines. The two male figures at the sides robed in golden vestments may be Old Testament prophets or possibly apostles thus bringing the total number of apostles depicted up to twelve.

Of particular importance is the lunette facing the entrance depicting a figure dressed in white, generally considered to be Saint Lawrence, advancing with decisive step towards a griddle enveloped in flames, holding an open book in his left hand and bearing a golden cross on his right shoulder. He resembles Christ with a golden halo around his head and with the cross on his shoulder as a sign of triumph, as testimony to his great faith expressed symbolically by the four gospels placed in the cabinet located on the left of the scene.

Located on the opposite side above the entrance door is the lunette of the Good Shepherd, a work of the greatest artistry. The figure of Christ dressed in regal purple and gold stands out in an idyllic landscape consisting of rocks, trees and shrubs with a morning sky in the background enlivened with varying shades of blue. He is dressed in regal purple and gold, seated between two groups of three sheep symmetrically arranged on each side (the one on the far left entirely the work of restoration).

Mausoleum of Galla Placidia

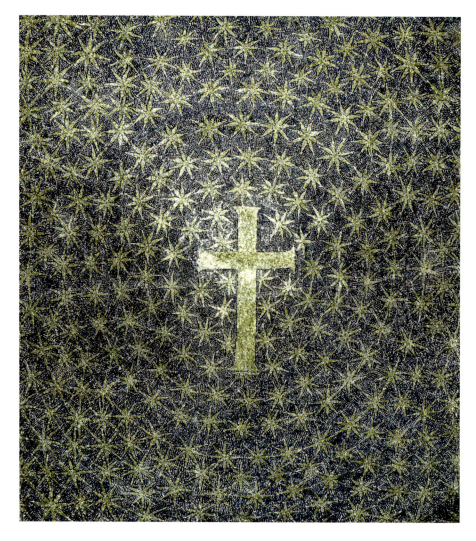

In the left hand Christ holds a cross and with the right hand he seems to caress the nose of a sheep stretching her head towards him.

The vaults and arches that surround the lunette are also decorated with elegant and beautiful designs consisting of single and double wave motifs, festoons of flowers and fruit, undulating waves and vine branches.

Particularly worthy of note is the floral decoration resembling a costly carpet covering the barrel vault of the northern and southern arms of the building. The whole surface is strewn with golden globes small white daisies, stylised roses alternating with large geometric flowers with indented petals similar to snowflakes. The entire design stands out on a background of indigo blue which gives the interior an atmosphere of subdued shade which is well-suited to a funerary building.

Justification for inclusion
in the World Heritage List

The Mausoleum of Galla Placidia is one of the most extraordinary monuments, in terms of architecture and decoration, which has come down to us intact from late antiquity. Without doubt one unusual feature is the fact that it was designed as an Imperial mausoleum but was not used as such but as a Christian sacellum, dedicated perhaps to Saint Lawrence, a martyr venerated in a particular way in Rome and the sphere of the Theodosian dynasty.

Although, as already mentioned, there is no certain documentary evidence concerning the purpose of the sacellum, many elements seem to support the hypothesis that it was intended as a sepulchre and conceived as a mausoleum for Galla Placidia and the imperial family: the pine cone at the top of the roof which is a typical funerary symbol, the subdued atmosphere of half-light inside created by the indigo blue of the mosaics, the light that barely enters through the small narrow windows and the iconography of the mosaics, all go to suggest that it was a sepulchre. The building deviates however from traditional imperial mausoleums on a central plan that are still extant or known from historical sources in the eastern part of the empire (Mausoleum of Galerius in Salonika, Mausoleum of Constantine in Constantinople, Mausoleum of Diocletian in Spalato) and the western part (Mausoleum of Saint Constance in Rome, Chapel of Saint Aquilinus in Milan) and is more akin to some of those mausoleums which, according to historical sources, were built in the Apostoleion of Constantinople, one of which (containing the sarcophagi of Arcadius, Eudoxia and Theodosius) must have had a cruciform plan. This design, breaking away from the more common type of imperial mausoleum on a circular plan, was to give a Christian meaning to imperial funerary architecture. The cruciform plan was then used extensively in numerous sacella of martyrs in northern Italy (Milan, Padua, Verona, Vicenza) and along the Adriatic coast (Rimini, Pola, etc.).

Another typical feature of western architectural tradition is the motif of the blind arches that run around all the external walls of the sacellum except for the façade. This feature can be seen not only in Ravenna in the Church of Santa Croce and the Basilica of Saint John the Evangelist (commissioned by Galla Placidia) but also in the contemporary Christian architecture of Milan, as for example in the Basilica of St. Simplicianus (late 4th century).

The exterior of the building is extremely simple and modest, in stark contrast to the sumptuous internal mosaic decoration made even more magnificent by the golden light filtering through the alabaster windows.

These are the most magnificent and beautiful mosaic wall decorations displaying the greatest artistry and symbolic significance that have come down to us.

Inside the sacellum and accustomed to its dim half-light, one is spellbound by the magnificence of the shapes, colours and beauty of the mosaic decorations that cover the vaults, arches, lunettes, cupola and embrasures of the windows, all vibrantly luminous, merging perfectly into the architecture and

Mausoleum of Galla Placidia

suggesting the idea of a universal space. The decorative concept that pervades the entire building, perhaps developed in centres of high culture such as Rome, Constantinople and Milan between the late 4th century and early 5th century, finds its highest expression in Ravenna, first in the Mausoleum of Galla Placidia and then in the Neonian Baptistery.

In both buildings the mosaics become a part of the architecture, merging with it, dissolving it and transforming it into light and colour to create an atmosphere far from the world outside. In our mausoleum the sky appears remote, deep and infinite as a result of precisely calculated illusions such as the stars around the cross decreasing in size as their concentric circles become smaller to convey a sense of depth.

The atmosphere is refined and magical at the same time, an ambience enhanced by the many elegant and exquisite decorations inspired at times by oriental silks and Sassanid art as for example in the floral decorations of the vaults in the northern and southern arms consisting of small golden spheres, small white daisies and large geometrical flowers with indented petals similar to snowflakes creating a two-dimensional decorative continuum bearing some resemblance to the mosaics on the ground floor of the Church of St. Sophia in Constantinople. The overall effect is that of being under a sumptuous pavilion adorned with fabrics of exotic origin stretching out to infinity.

The architectural parts in the mausoleum are therefore no longer marked by sculpted friezes – as for example in the contemporary Basilica of S. Maria Maggiore in Rome - but by ornamental strips in the mosaic, similar to cornices, which seem to obey the rigid rules of spatial distribution. In fact all the curved surfaces of the vaults and the cupola are covered with ornamental features while human figures are to be seen in the lunettes.

From the stylistic viewpoint, the mosaics of the mausoleum contain features not to be seen elsewhere, not in Rome, nor Milan, Campania and Greece, which were to become peculiar to the mosaic production of Ravenna. The human figures are well-formed with a volume and plasticity uncommon to western pictorial art of late antiquity. The edges of the figures are clearly defined, as are the folds in the clothing which is in stark contrast to contemporary mosaics of

MAUSOLEUM OF GALLA PLACIDIA

Rome (Santa Maria Maggiore), conceived and produced with a rather impressionistic technique, and of Milan (St Aquilinus) where it is colouristic effects that prevail.

The legacy of Hellenistic Roman art is clearly expressed in the figures of the apostles represented here with lively plasticity as in the postures of ancient philosophers. Dressed in white tunics and pallia, they stand out against the dark blue background with their right hands raised solemnly, almost as a Christian translation of imperial dignitaries proclaiming the victorious emperor.

Another example of how Christian art appropriated images and motifs from high classical art and gave them new symbolic meanings is the mosaic of doves which represent the souls of the dead drinking the water of divine grace.

The theme is however much more ancient; suffice it to say that it was Pliny the Elder in his Natural History that mentioned the name of a Greek mosaic. Sosos of Pergamum (Asia Minor), who lived in the second century before Christ, became very famous for having created a mosaic of doves perched on the edge of a vase. Copies from the Roman period of this mosaic composition have come down to us, the most famous being the emblem of the floor mosaic of Hadrian's Villa in Tivoli, now in the Capitoline Museum of Rome.

The mosaic of greatest artistry and which more than any other reveals the continuity of the classical tradition in the art of Ravenna is the Good Shepherd lunette above the entrance.

The image of a beardless Christ, his face framed by long brown hair that falls onto his shoulders, has suggested a comparison with Apollo while the position and twisting of his body has been compared to the mythical Orpheus.

The figures of this pastoral scene are set

Mausoleum of Galla Placidia

in an idyllic landscape of rocks, trees and shrubs in delicate tones of green, blue and brown which stand out against the blue background sky typical of the Hellenistic tradition.

The composition is extremely refined with elements distributed artistically and in accordance with principles of symmetry. The Good Shepherd at the centre is surrounded by two groups of three sheep arranged symmetrically on either side all facing the mystical shepherd set in a landscape with carefully graded colours designed to create an illusion of depth.

This scene represents a turning point in Christian iconography as the Good Shepherd is no longer depicted as in the western catacombs or sarcophagi of the third and fourth centuries with a short tunic and *pedum* (crook), but now in imperial attire with a gold tunic and purple mantle due to the influence of imperial ceremony, courtly art and the close ties established between Ravenna and Constantinople during this period.

The subject of the Good Shepherd is particularly appropriate for a mausoleum since the ancient liturgies allude to the departed as being sheep accepted by Christ into his fold. Moreover, the position of Christ above the entrance symbolises the doorway to eternal life, the gateway to the kingdom of heaven after death.

An unusual feature is the representation in the same building of the Good Shepherd and St. Lawrence who is depicted for the first time with great realism next to the grating on which he was martyred. In the second half of the sixth century, on the triumphal arch of the Basilica of St. Lawrence outside the walls of Rome the saint was still presented however as a deacon, holding a cross and an open book, a fact that underlines the originality of the mosaic in this mausoleum.

Another fact of importance is that the entire iconographic scheme seems to have a sole purpose, suggesting the concept that through faith in Christ, which constitutes the gateway to eternal life, through the sacrifice exemplified by the martyrdom of St. Lawrence and the works of the apostles, one can obtain that salvation which finds its greatest exaltation in the apocalyptic cross, symbol of Christ's second coming, acclaimed by the apostles and proclaimed by the four living beings of the apocalypse. All the other funerary symbols also allude to hope in eternal life.

The glory of the cross thus appears in a cosmic unity. Similar apocalyptic representations emphasising the divine nature of Christ are widespread in the west and especially in Rome (mosaic in the apse of St. Pudenziana, triumphal arch of S. Maria Maggiore) even if set in different iconographic contexts. If the mausoleum was commissioned by Galla Placidia, who sensitive to the questions of Christian spirituality in her times, one may presume that such a complex and articulate decorative scheme was suggested by St. Peter Chrysologus, her advisor and theologian. All the decoration is in fact an expression of her faith in orthodoxy and the apocalyptic iconography of the cross and the four living beings accent not the first coming of Christ but the second, and therefore his divine nature which was played down by some heretical groups such as the Nestorians and even more by the Arians. The presence of imperial iconography expresses the influence of the court of Constantinople over Ravenna in this period.

According to some experts it is probable that for the composition of mosaics of such high artistic quality, master craftsmen were brought in from Constantinople, helped obviously by local craftsmen. This would have taken place in the context of the bonds and artistic cooperation established between Ravenna and Constantinople at the time of Galla Placidia.

5TH CENTURY

Neonian (Orthodox) Baptistery

Historical Background

The baptistery stands to the north of the present day cathedral of Ravenna which in the early seventeen hundreds replaced the older Ursian Basilica commissioned by the bishop Ursus in the early fifth century and after whom it was named. The baptistery can probably be attributed to the same bishop though no precise information about its founding has come down to us.

At the time of the bishop Neonius (ca. 450-475) it underwent substantial renovation which, among other things, brought about the reconstruction of the upper part with a cupola and entire redecoration of the interior. For these reasons it is known as the Ursian Baptistery, or Neonian Baptistery, or Baptistery of the Catholic Cathedral, to distinguish it from that of the Arian cathedral.

In the 7th century, at the time of the bishop Theodorus (677-688), a great bronze cross (now kept inside the baptistery) was placed at the top of the roof. In the 12th century the floor was raised as a part of extensive works inside (such as truncating the bases of the arches).

Between 1566 and 1573 at the time of Cardinal Giulio Feltrio della Rovere, more work was done on the floor and the walled-up windows were reopened taking on a new rectangular form.

The building of a new vicarage at the beginning of the 17th century next to the baptistery resulted in the demolition of the two apses on the south-east and south-west sides. Toward the middle of the 19th century substantial restoration work on the mosaics was done by Felice Kibel, a restorer from Rome whose methods and results are now highly questionable.

The decade 1870-1880 was a period of digs, research, projects and work supervised by the architect Lanciani which led to the discovery of the original baptismal font on the perimeter of which the present font stands. An elevation of the building was also proposed but not carried out.

Between 1899 and 1906 a new restoration programme was begun on the mosaics as well as the marble and stucco decorations. In the nineteen sixties and eighties also new inspections and research were done to study the state of conservation of the building.

Description

The building, constructed in brick on an octagonal plan, cannot be seen in its original proportions as it is now interred by some 3 metres. It has alternating straight sides and sides with apses opened in the upper level by windows with round arches.

Above the arches the brickwork is relieved by pilasters that join at the top in a series of double suspended arches. It is interesting to note how on the north-west side a piece of sculpture from a Roman sarcophagus depicting a horseman holding a crown of victory has been reused.

The entrance door opens on the west side and the lintel, an architrave dating from the 16th century, bears the inscription "En espoir Dieu".

The interior, in which there are four apses, is articulated in two rows of arches one above the other, leading to the cupola made out of two concentric rings of terracotta piping decreasing in diameter towards the top and thus giving a semblance of great lightness. The internal decoration is sumptuous consisting of marble in the lower part, stuccowork in the middle section and mosaics in the top level.

In order to suit the architectural structure of the cupola, the mosaic composition was divided into three distinct zones; a central medallion and two concentric bands.

The central medallion is decorated with a scene of the baptism of Christ which is highly appropriate to the building's func-

Neonian (Orthodox) Baptistery

tion. The naked figure of the Saviour stands waist deep in the transparent waters of the Jordan which is personified by as an old man holding a reed in his left hand and a green cloth in his right for the purpose of drying Christ after the rite. The Baptist, standing on a rock jutting into the river, administers the baptism holding a cup above Christ's head with his right hand. A dove representing the Holy Spirit can be seen descending from on high. The scene is set in a golden background which becomes lighter in the area around Christ's head, the dove and above the Baptist's head due to unsuccessful restoration work done just after the middle of the 19th century.

The first inner band surrounding the medallion depicts the twelve apostles against a dark blue background, slowly advancing with same dignified rhythmic step in two processions led by Peter and Paul. In their hands, covered by a pallium, they all carry a gold crown which symbolises victory. They are dressed in tunics and pallia coloured alternately white and gold and are separated by elegant floral candelabras which also confer a sense of movement and rotation. The wider outer band, subdivided by large acanthus plants into eight architectural sections with niches containing alternately thrones and altars, alludes to the concept of the heavenly city.

The thrones are flanked by gardens of plants and flowers behind transepts while the altars stand between two empty chairs. Like the thrones symbolising imperial power depicted on late Byzantine coinage, the thrones in this mosaic which are surmounted by a purple cushion and a small cross, express the concept of the Etimasia or "preparation of

Neonian (Orthodox) Baptistery

God's throne of judgement" (Book of Revelation. Ch. 4). The altars, on each of which is placed a gospel, also have a symbolic meaning alluding to Christ and the diffusion of Christian doctrine while the viridarium (herb garden) located at the sides of the thrones suggest heavenly gardens and the empty chairs on either side of the thrones are reserved by Christ for the elect. In the upper drum supporting the cupola at the level of the eight windows there is an ornate stucco decoration, once polychrome, dating from the period of Neonius (451-475). Below the stucco and between the windows there are columns and niches which contain the figures of sixteen prophets each holding a scroll or codex. The lunettes above the niches are decorated in stucco with pairs of animals facing each other alternating with scenes from the Old and New Testaments such as the *Traditio Legis*, Daniel in the lion's den, Jonah and a youthful Christ stepping on a lion and snake. In the lower part between the arches figures dressed in white, probably prophets, stand enveloped in acanthus on a dark blue background. The four apses, now without any stucco decoration, must have been covered with scenes depicting respectively Christ walking on water, Christ washing the disciples' feet, the healing of the paralytic and an idyllic pastoral scene with regenerative water alluding to baptism as inferred by the inscriptions which, although remade in the 19th century, can still be read.

Justification for inclusion in the World Heritage List

The Neonian Baptistery is the only one of its kind in the ambit of early Christian art because no other baptismal building in the world of late antiquity has preserved its architectural structure and internal decoration of marble, stucco and mosaics in such a perfect state of conservation. As regards the architecture, the Baptistery is known for its octagonal plan, a feature common to many baptismal buildings in northern Italy and the Adriatic area. An unusual feature is the great cupola with clay tubes, a western system of construction, anticipating a larger version of this technique found in San Vitale. As corroboration of the uniqueness of this building one only has to consider some of the oldest baptisteries of the 4th and 5th centuries built at Antioch, Constantinople, Ephesus, Trier, Aquileia, Milan, Rome and many other cities where often the sole extant remains are the foundations or outer walls.

The mosaic decoration, which is so complex and well-conserved, has no precedents.

Only a small part of the mosaics decorating the Baptistery of Naples (late 4th early 5th centuries) have survived: a small monogrammatic golden cross occupies a dominant position at the centre of the cupola on a background of blue sky sprinkled with golden stars while on the pendentives and walls there are only a few fragmentary scenes (apostles, living beings of the apocalypse, the wedding in Cana, the good shepherd, etc.).

Remains of mosaic decoration of a later period (early 6th century) can still be seen in the Baptistery of Albenga in the vault of a niche decorated with Christ's monogram surrounded by twelve doves on a blue background sprinkled with white stars. The lunette underneath is decorated with two lambs facing a cross, festoons of leaves, ornamental motifs and inscriptions. These decorations however have limited chromatic range since the basic colours are mainly blue and white.

These comparisons underscore the exceptional nature of the mosaic decorations of

Neonian (Orthodox) Baptistery

the Neonian Baptistery which represents the oldest example of a scene of Christ's baptism in mosaic in a historic building that has come down to us. Earlier examples can be found only in the third century catacombs and some 4th century sarcophagi.

The influence of classical art is also evident in the personalisation of the river Jordan as an old person holding out a cloth for Christ to dry himself, and also in the realistic representation of Christ's body naked.

The influence of Hellenic-Roman art is nevertheless present not only in the band of mosaics with imitated architectural features which might bring to mind the frescoes of Pompei, but especially in the procession of the twelve apostles where a certain dynamic vigour can be seen in the human figure combined with great realism in the facial expressions.

The scene of the twelve apostles, which represents "the most grandiose expression of Christian art", are on a large scale and in their statuesque poses they bring to mind classical statues: the body appears moulded while the faces have such distinctive fea-

Neonian (Orthodox) Baptistery

tures as to be considered among the best examples of Roman portraiture.

The qualitative level of these mosaics, believed to be the highest artistic expression that has come down to us from late antiquity, demonstrates that there must have been master craftsmen in Ravenna with skills of the highest order at the time of Neonius and their presence can be explained only in relation to the imperial court at Ravenna.

Indeed imperial models inspired the iconography of the apostles who offer golden crowns with hands veiled by garments, harking back to the tradition of the *aurum coronarium* offered by defeated peoples to the victors, or even the emperor himself.

Yet another unique feature of the mosaics in the cupola is the vast highly graded chromatic range with subtle shades of green, blue, pink, violet, grey and white juxtaposed with great pictorial sensitivity which is not matched by any other mosaic in Ravenna or elsewhere.

Overall the colour tones are bright and the light, which is almost like night inside the mausoleum of Galla Placidia, here becomes like morning. In this atmosphere of pure light and colour the catechumens received the *illuminatio*, by which they became neophytes and as such were ready to become members of the Church.

One should also notice the perfect fusion of mosaic decoration and architecturally defined space which is a characteristic feature of the historic buildings of Ravenna. The mosaics become a part of the architecture and partly replace it. The floral candelabras form imaginary ribs in the cupola while the architecture represented in perspective in the mosaics almost conceal the walls. One has the impression of an unreal space in which the walls seem to dematerialise and dissolve in the colour and light.

The compositional scheme of the cupola had already been used more than a century earlier in the cupola of the Mausoleum of Centcelles near to Tarragona (Spain), or in the famous Rotunda at Salonika in Greece and also Constantine's Mausoleum in Rome (middle of the 4th century). Here in Ravenna the scheme has been masterfully adapted to a baptistery. The whole cupola seems to rotate like a wheel around its fixed centre, the medallion.

This rotary movement, suggested by the various decorative elements such as the floral candelabras, the drapes around the medallion and the alternating colours of white and gold of the apostles' garments, gives the impression that the dome is expanding to infinity with a movement which, to quote Dante (Paradise XIV, 1) goes "from the centre to the circle" and "from the circle to the centre", like the endless rotation of celestial bodies.

The scene of Christ's baptism is set on a background of the celestial city and the apostles offering gold crowns with compositional and stylistic solutions of the highest artistic level.

All these features make one think that there is a unifying concept in the work of a single master well acquainted with the language of glorification, a language dense with doctrinal meanings, expressing the complete adherence of Ravenna to the strictest principles of the orthodox faith.

The building therefore has unique features, as seen above in regard to architecture and the stucco and mosaic decorations, that distinguish it from all other early Christian baptisteries in the West and near East.

5TH CENTURY

Arian Baptistery

Historical Background

This baptistery, built by Theodoric (493 – 526) next to the Arian Cathedral, was confiscated after the Byzantine reconquest together with all the other buildings dedicated to Arian worship, and was reconsecrated in the Orthodox faith (AD 561); it thus became an oratory dedicated to the Virgin Mary.

During the period of Exarchate rule the monks of St. Basil set up a religious community alongside it which they called Santa Maria in Cosmedin for the beauty of its decorations.

In the eleventh century the building was taken over by Benedictine monks who made it particularly prestigious and remained there until 1441.

From the middle of the fifteenth century the oratory of Santa Maria in Cosmedin was turned over to the secular clergy and Pope Eugene IV (1431-1447) who placed it in the hands of Cardinal Bessarion of Trebisond, a benefice that later passed to numerous prelates or Abbots incumbent.

In the 16th century the brothers Baldassar and Corradi Grassi of Bologna were made the beneficiaries and important restoration work done at that time is due to them.

In the second half of the 17th century a new building was built onto the west face referred to as "The oratory of the Cross" of which the former baptistery became the apse and so its original appearance was lost for many centuries.

After passing into the hands of private families in the nineteenth century it was only in 1914 that it finally became property of the state. Since then the Superintendency for Environmental and Architectural Heritage of Ravenna has tried to restore it to its original state with numerous restoration works.

Description

The baptistery, situated on the south-west side of the Arian Cathedral but aligned with it, stands as a small brick building on an octagonal plan consisting of four flat sides alternating with four projecting apses, one of which on the east side is larger than the others.

The building cannot be seen in its original proportions since it has sunk by some 2.31 metres into the ground.

A cornice divides the building externally into two parts. The top part covered by a cupola opens on each side with a semi-circular arched window while in the lower part the four apses protrude each covered by a small roof under which there is a serrated cornice and on the north-western side the entrance door.

Originally the baptistery would have had a more articulate architecture as suggested by excavations between 1916 and 1919 by Gerola which revealed an ambulatory in the form of a ring-shaped corridor about 1.90 metres wide running around seven sides of the building and leaving open only the side with the main apse facing east. The only remains of this visible today are the junctures in the perimeter wall on the right of the eastern apse built by Gerola himself during restoration work to suggest the presence of the ambulatory.

The brick walls inside are completely bare without plaster, marble or mosaic, remains of which however were uncovered beneath the present floor in the excavations of 1969.

The only decorated part is in the cupola which is covered with mosaics generally inspired by those of the Neonian Baptistery (of the Catholic Cathedral) but with simplified decorations perhaps due to reasons of limited space and with variations intended to convey different meanings.

In the Arian Baptistery the central medallion depicting the baptismal scene of Christ is surrounded by two wide mosaic bands as in the preceding Neonian Baptistery but only once concentric band, perhaps due again to limitations of space.

In the centre a young beardless Christ stands up to his waist in the transparent waters of the Jordan, personified on his right in the form of an old man with a full beard and long hair seated next to an upturned amphora from which the river's waters flow. He holds a reed and on his head, the claws of a lobster symbolising the personification of the river.

Standing on Christ's left is John the Baptist wearing a large camel skin tunic. He holds his right hand over Christ's head while a dove symbolising the Holy Spirit descends from above and anoints Christ with an issue of divine spirit.

The composition is well-balanced and the figures seem to fill the space harmoniously, adapting to the circular medallion.

The large concentric band is occupied by the apostles all carrying a crown symbolising martyrdom and triumph in their hands veiled by their pallia. They are divided into two groups led respectively by Peter holding the keys and Paul holding the scrolls of the divine law who meet before a great throne covered with a purple cushion on which a jewelled cross stands.

Technical and scientific research made it possible to ascertain that the mosaics belong to two different chronological periods: the central medallion with the scene of Christ's baptism, the throne, the figure of Saint Peter, Saint Paul and the apostles who follow them are of the period of Theodoric (493-526) while the remaining apostles were probably completely redone towards the middle of the 6th century, a hypothesis supported also by the style and use of different materials.

Justification for inclusion in the World Heritage List

No other city in the world with remains from late antiquity has managed to preserve a baptistery dedicated to the Arian cult with mosaic decorations – very similar only in appearance to those of the Catholic baptistery – that enable us to gain a better understanding of Arianism and reveal some of the basic aspects that distinguish this from orthodox doctrine.

Together with the Arian Cathedral it is located in the "Gothic" quarter in the northeastern part of the city set apart from the Catholic area, a fact that testifies to the clear separation between the Latin and Gothic religious communities during the reign of Theodoric.

As regards the type of architecture, this building is something of a rarity among all the early Christian baptisteries on an octagonal plan, which were very numerous in Italy during the 5th and 6th centuries, due to the presence of an ambulatory. This structure was probably built for precise liturgical purposes connected with the Arian cult and cannot be reconstructed due to the paucity of documentary sources.

From the viewpoint of iconography the mosaic decoration is of the utmost interest.

Without doubt the general scheme reflects that of the Neonian Baptistery, but the differences to be found cannot be attributed only to the limited space as often claimed but to the desire to express religious concepts quite distinct from those of orthodox faith.

Since the mosaic decorations reflect the ideology of the time and the political-religious ideas of their patrons, it is very likely that the differences in the iconographic scheme of the Arian Baptistery were intended to stress different concepts of their faith and thus the singular principles of the Arian religion, such as the physical nature and humanity of Christ subordinate to the Father, the only God.

While in the Neonian (Catholic) Baptistery the twelve apostles with their crowns held in hands veiled by their garments acclaim Christ in the central medallion, proclaimed during the baptismal rite as Son of God and therefore recognised as divine as the second person of the trinity, in the Arian Baptistery the apostles pay homage to the great jewelled throne which is right on the other side of the baptism scene and on which a cross rests with a purple sudarium draped over its arms.

In this case the throne is not to be interpreted as apocalyptic and a symbol of the *Etimasia*, prepared therefore for Christ on the day of universal judgement or as a generic image of the sovereignty of Christ, or as an apparition of the sign of the Son of Man in the eschatological sense, but rather as an expression of the physical nature of Christ and his suffering on the cross as a human being, coherent with Arian belief and in antithesis to the orthodox dogma which stressed both the human and divine nature of Christ.

Another noticeable feature is the location of the throne opposite the baptism scene in the central medallion. It is quite probable that it also corresponds to the position in which the bishop sat so that the person being baptised, facing east and looking

Arian Baptistery

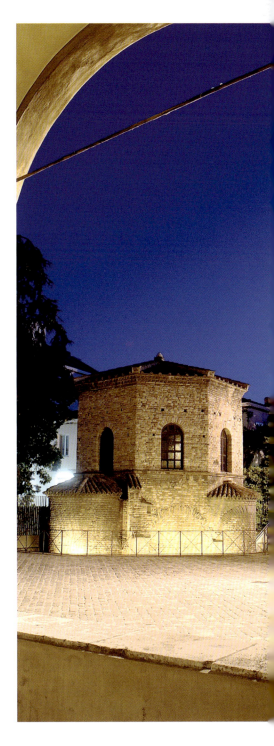

up would have been able to contemplate Christ's throne with its cross, the symbol of death and resurrection.

The theme of victory over death is however dear to the symbolism of baptism, a rite assimilated into the initiation, purification and rebirth of the Christian within the Church.

From the viewpoint of iconography, a feature of particular interest for its uniqueness in decorative mosaic art, as in the Neonian Baptistery moreover, is the depiction of Christ naked with anatomical details represented with great realism.

Differences between the two baptisteries can be seen also from the stylistic viewpoint. The indigo blue background of the Neonian Baptistery becomes gold in the Arian Baptistery where the figures seem more immobile and abstract.

For the first time in the mosaics of Ravenna, the apostles are depicted with halos and solemn faces represented from a frontal perspective. The figures appear flat and rigid, defined by marked lines of delineation, the chromatic range is reduced and simplified while the faces appear less realistic, almost transfigured into metaphysical beings.

The twelve apostles, produced by a number of different mosaicists, separated by stylised palms to indicate that the scene is set in heaven, are depicted moving forward slowly in the same pose, with the same gestures and even the same folds in their garments. The iteration of these elements confers a perfect sense of compositional unity and rhythm. Finally, a detail worthy of note is the glistening golden surface of the background, without any spatial features, which confers an unreal and transcendent dimension and expresses a more advanced process of abstraction.

LATE 5TH EARLY 6TH CENTURY

Basilica of Sant'Apollinare Nuovo

Historical Background

The Basilica of Sant'Apollinare Nuovo, built by Theodoric (493-526) between the end of the 5th century and the early 6th century. It was dedicated to Christ according to a no longer extant inscription referred to by Andreas Agnellus (*Liber Pontificalis Ecclesia Ravennatis*) which was in the apse of the church and which read as follows: "Theodoricus rex hanc eclesiam a fundamentis in nomine domini nostri Jesu Christi fecit" ("King Theodoric had this church built from its foundations and dedicated it to the name of Jesus Christ our Lord).

Standing next to the palace rebuilt by the Gothic king it would have been used as a palatine basilica and it can be considered the most prestigious of the Arian churches.

After the Byzantine reconquest and consecration to the orthodox faith which occurred after Justinian's edict of AD 561, its patron became St. Martin of Tours, famed for his staunch opposition to heresies and to Arianism in particular. It became known as St. Martin of the Golden Sky on account of the splendour its ceiling in gilt casements.

Considerable but negatively criticised restoration work was started on the mosaics in the middle of the nineteenth century by the restorer from Rome, Felice Kibel.

In 1950 the baroque apse was screened off with an apse wall that traced the original perimeter. This was then demolished between 1986 and 1996 to make the baroque apse visible again which can now be seen completely restored.

DESCRIPTION

The basilica is characterised by great architectural simplicity: built in brick, its façade has a tympanum framed by two pilaster strips and pierced by a mullioned window with two small windows above.

Two rows of twelve columns in Greek marble divide the interior into three naves of considerable length ending in a semicircular apse. However, the original layout cannot be seen due to the numerous alterations made over the centuries.

In the sixteenth century, due to a rise in the underlying water table the floor was raised by about 1.2 metres bringing it to street level. To do this the columns and arches were raised from the old floor and the strip of wall between the arches and the first band of mosaics, almost certainly decorated with polychrome stucco, was removed.

The ancient apse, the foundations of which were discovered during the restoration work of 1895 was semicircular internally and polygonal externally, and constructed in clay tubes and therefore quite different to the current apse, which is longer, dating from the baroque period.

A fine collection of liturgical marbles is kept in the basilica including a veined Greek marble pulpit, openwork screens with elegant decorative and symbolic motifs, a low parapet decorated with two peacocks facing a vase above which a cross stands, four red porphyry columns with typically Byzantine capitals originally belonging to a ciborium and a small four-pillared rectangular altar. The interior of the basilica must have been

Basilica of Sant'Apollinare Nuovo

decorated sumptuously with marbles in the lower part, stuccos in the middle part (which disappeared in the works of the 16th century) and mosaics in the upper part which must have covered not only the walls but also the apse, triumphal arch and the interior façade.

The only surviving decorations are the mosaics covering the walls of the central nave in three parallel bands attributable partly to the period of Theodoric and modifications made during Justinian's reign.

The top band depicts scenes of Christ's miracles and parables with passion scenes on the left and post resurrection scenes on the right. The middle band depicts white-robed male figures, probably prophets, with nimbus and holding scrolls or finely bound books. The lower band is decorated with a long procession of martyrs and virgins (from the time of Justinian) and a representation of the *Palatium* of Theodoric, the *Civitas Classe* and Christ and the Virgin seated on a throne between four archangels (period of Theodoric).

The Christological scenes occupy 26 panels, thirteen on each side interspersed repeatedly with the same motif, which becomes a common separating element between one scene and the next, consisting of a hieratic shell below a cross, flanked by two doves and from which a jewelled crown hangs above the head of the persons depicted in the mosaic band underneath.

On the left wall – in order from the apse toward to the entrance – the following episodes are depicted: the miracle of the loaves (due to an erroneous restoration but originally the transformation of water into wine at the Wedding at Cana), the miracle of the loaves and fish, the calling of Peter and Andrew, the healing of the blind at Jericho, the healing of the woman with an issue of blood, the Samaritan at the well, the resurrection of Lazarus, the parable of the Pharisee and the publican, the widow's mite, Christ in judgement separating the sheep from the goats, the healing of the paralytic at Capernaum, driving out evil spirits (the demons enter pigs that rush into the lake), the healing of the paralytic at Bethesda.

The scenes depicted on the right wall are: the last supper, praying in the garden of Gethsemane, Judas' kiss, Jesus before the High Priests, Jesus before Caiaphas, Peter's denial foretold, Peter's denial, Judas returns the betrayal money, Jesus before Pontius Pilate, Jesus on the way to Calvary, the women at the tomb, disciples on the road to Emmaus, the incredulity of Thomas.

The episodes of the Christological series use different artistic languages depending on the various concepts that they are intended to express.

The scenes depicting the miracles and parables of Christ are typified by the presence of few but essential hieratic personages which is appropriate for a miraculous event. Christ is always young, beardless and dressed in purple. The naturalistic elements are reduced to a minimum and the landscapes are set in a gold background.

The scenes depicting the passion and after the resurrection are instead more crowded and dramatic, with more realistic rendering. Christ is depicted as old and bearded with a pained expression in keeping with a passion scene.

At the beginning of the lower band on the right wall there are scenes depicting the *Palatium* of Theodoric in front of buildings of the city of Ravenna in the Catholic and Arian Episcopal complex.

The palace is in the form of a central peristyle surmounted by a gable in which Theodoric mounted on a horse would have been depicted. Two wings with porticos flank the central peristyle with small winged victories holding up festoons decorating the spaces above the columns. The spaces between the columns is decorated with elegant curtains tied back or knotted at the centre which during the reign of Justinian replaced the images of personages most probably connected with the Arian church or court no longer appreciated in the new historical situation. This purification of the mosaics from Arian concepts took place at the time

BASILICA OF SANT'APOLLINARE NUOVO

of Bishop Agnellus when the church was reconsecrated to the Catholic faith. Traces of some of these personages have remained as the hands or forearms, clearly visible on four of the columns while above the curtains the outline of their heads can be seen.

A procession of 26 martyrs leads from the palace toward the apse. Each martyr identified by a name written above the head is depicted with a halo and carries a gold crown in veiled hands. These saints, dressed in white and separated from each other by thin stylised palms, stand out on a golden background and walk on green meadow with flowers led by Saint Martin distinguished by the purple mantle over his white robe. They proceed towards an enthroned Christ in a beneficent attitude, flanked by four archangels.

On the left wall opposite the palace and the city of Ravenna is the *Civitas Classis*. The city with its monuments is depicted with high city walls and three ships riding the waves outside the entrance to the port, one with sails lowered. The outline of personages can be seen on the city walls. These were removed by Bishop Agnellus and replaced with a background of golden tesseras. From this point the procession of saints and the three kings proceeds towards the enthroned virgin. Every saint, dressed opulently, carries a gold crown.

The figure of the Madonna, flanked by four archangels, faces the figure of Christ depicted in all his majesty on the opposite wall. In contrast her tall slender figure and wide open eyes convey a sense of great hieratic importance. The mosaics of Sant'Apollinare Nuovo were thus produced in two different periods, the reigns of Theodoric and of Justinian, and characterised by different materials and craftsmanship.

Justification for inclusion in the World Heritage List

At the end of the 5th century a harmonic fusion of architectural and decorative elements was created in Sant'Apollinare Nuovo, some of eastern origin and others from the west which was to become a distinctive feature of the building and art of Ravenna, quite different from that of contemporary early Christian basilicas elsewhere in the West.

The plan of the basilica is extremely long in line with the customary architecture of the West and would have ended in an apse with semicircular interior and polygonal exterior wall in the style of other examples in Constantinople and the Aegean. Its structure is of clay piping while the walls are in brickwork thus continuing the western tradition. The pilaster strips in the lower side walls are connected by a cornice which then incorporates the windows and is very reminiscent of Syrian churches. The columns were imported from Constantinople and bear the mark of Greek manufacturers, like the elegant lyre-shaped capitals, the pulpit and the choir screens which form a part of the priceless liturgical furnishings of the building.

The abundance of such a costly material in the architecture and Greek marble sculptures is explained not only by the connection with the importance of the palatine building which would also have had a beautiful marble inlay floor, but mainly in terms of the good political relations between Theodoric and the Emperor of Constantinople who adopted Theodoric as a son and acknowledged him as King of Italy.

The originality of the basilica lies not only in these considerations but also in its architectural proportions, the light that filters inside and the magnificent mosaics which are completely different to those of contemporary basilicas in Rome.

While a typical feature of the mosaic decorations of the oldest Roman churches (for example, Santa Maria Maggiore, St. Paul Outside the Walls) was the use of single mosaic panels arranged in one or more rows, in Sant'Apollinare Nuovo a long procession of saints moves towards the apse with a new kind of rhythmic sense.

The mosaic decorations of Sant'Apollinare

Basilica of Sant'Apollinare Nuovo

Nuovo, a large part of which have survived, are of exceptional interest as they help us to understand the evolution of Byzantine wall mosaics from the age of Theodoric to that of Justinian in terms of iconography, style and ideology. In fact it is easy to see the influence of the Arian religion and politics of Theodoric as well as the Byzantine and orthodox Catholic reaction.

The 26 Christological scenes, dating from the period of Theodoric, represent the greatest New Testament series and of those done in mosaic, are the oldest that have come down to us.

Mention should be made of the fact that in the series of miracles the scenes do not follow a precise chronological order and important episodes of the life of Christ were left out, while there are others that constitute a *unicum* in early Christian art such as the parable of 'the Pharisee and the publican' 'the healing of the paralytic at Capernaum' or at least very rare examples such as 'the healing of the two blind men of Jericho' or 'the widow's mite'. Other scenes such as 'the calling of Peter and Andrew' and 'the healing of the demoniac' have no precedents in earlier art for the originality of compositional scheme.

In the Passion series the scenes of the flagellation and the crucifixion are notable by their absence as they would have been considered too degrading for the sensibility of early Christians.

Of particular interest from the iconographical viewpoint is the panel of 'the last supper', described by Van Berchem and Clouzot as "one of the oldest representations of this scene, many times reworked by artists from the Middle Ages to the Renaissance".

In accordance with Roman custom, the apostles, instead of being seated, recline around a semicircular triclinium on which there are two fish and some loaves of bread. Christ is seated on the left in the place of honour while Judas is on the far right.

Some experts believe that the presence of the fish instead of the paschal lamb is a representation of the 'meal of the pure' celebrated by Jews on Friday evening, a practice which spread to the Arians who believed that Jesus too would have eaten thus before the Passion.

The Christological series of Sant'Apollinare is therefore unique in its choice of themes and the succession of scenes that evidently reflect the religious concepts of the Goths.

Since the Arians considered Christ as above all a teacher, guide and example to follow and imitate in order to obtain salvation, those scenes that best express these concepts were represented (the calling of Peter and Andrew, the blind men of Jericho, and the demon-possessed man who followed the teacher immediately after the miracles) or the dogmas of the Arian faith such as subordination of the Son to the Father expressed in the episode of the resurrection of Lazarus in which, according to the text of John's Gospel (John 11. 41-42), Christ prays to the Father for permission to perform the miracle.

These mosaic panels must have been saved from the purging during Justinian's reign as these scenes must not have been considered offensive to orthodox sensibilities as they could also be interpreted in accordance with orthodox dogma.

The mosaics of Theodoric's period are also an expression of a culture that was certainly influenced by the world of Constantinople as can be seen from the presence of numerous iconographical elements of Imperial provenance.

In the Christological series of panels the Teacher is not dressed in the usual clothes of early Christian iconography but wears purple, just as the Virgin and Christ seated

Basilica of Sant'Apollinare Nuovo

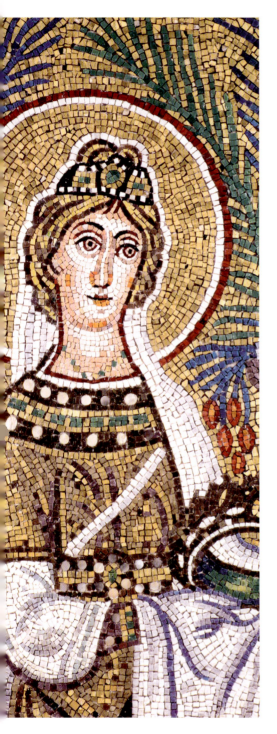

on the throne in the lower band wear regal attire. They are flanked by four archangels, seen full face and standing immobile, that draw inspiration from the four *ostarii* of the Byzantine court who were guards of the Imperial throne.

The image of the enthroned Madonna and Child is the oldest monumental image of the Virgin that has come down to us and therefore constitutes a prototype for countless depictions of the Virgin in majesty to be found in Byzantine and Medieval art.

What is quite unique and completely original for early Christian art is the representation of the city of Ravenna, with its sacred *Palatium* and the city of Classe with its port, inside a religious building and thus evoking an otherworldly dimension. Such an unusual choice for those times, and indeed for many centuries after, can perhaps be explained by the desire to glorify Theodoric within a religious building through two great centres of power, the palace and the city of Classe with its port connecting the city with the East and in particular Constantinople. In this way it was intended to underline the role of Ravenna as heir and successor to Rome which the Gothic king happily ruled.

This ideological message was expressed clearly by images removed by the Byzantine *damnatio memoriae*. In fact in the gable of the *Palatium* Theodoric was originally depicted on horseback flanked by the personifications of Rome Ravenna and Ravenna, the latter having the right foot on the sea and the left foot on land.

The purging done by the Catholics, with the intention of eliminating all references to the period of Ostrogoth domination and the Arian religion, was also concerned with the reinforcement of orthodox Catholic concepts. Leading the procession of saints St. Martin, the proud antagonist of the Arians, stands out while the procession of virgins is led by St.

BASILICA OF SANT'APOLLINARE NUOVO

Euphemia, the valiant supporter of the ideas of the Council of Chalcedon (451) which had stressed the double nature of Christ. The dogma of the trinity, understood in its anti-Arian significance, is also expressed in the figures of the Magi adoring Christ as God.

In Sant'Apollinare Nuovo the co-existence of mosaic decorations dating in part from the late 5th and early 6th centuries and in part from the second half of the 6th century makes it possible to follow the development of mosaics in Ravenna from the period of Theodoric to that of Justinian and also stylistic developments.

The mosaics of Theodoric's period depict figures in a fairly natural way, characterised by various poses and postures and the use of colour shades that are still quite soft, especially the monumental figures of the prophets located between the windows, represented in flowing lines and in various poses and postures. The landscape background exists alongside the golden background which would become the dominant colour only later in the Justinian period.

It is in fact to this period that the processions in the lower band belong, the processions of the martyrs and the virgins which are the highest expression of orthodoxy in the Byzantine "high style".

The male and female saints, from the East and the West, bear witness to the universality of the orthodox faith by their heterogeneous provenance. Proceeding with the same pace and rhythm they form a long procession which appears to wend its way towards the infinite, without beginning and without end. The sacred images also express the highest values of Byzantine aesthetics: light, colour and rhythm. Flattened on a golden transcendental background, two-dimensional and linear, wearing precious garments, they seem to have lost all sense of the human earthly world and are projected completely into a metaphysical transcendental dimension.

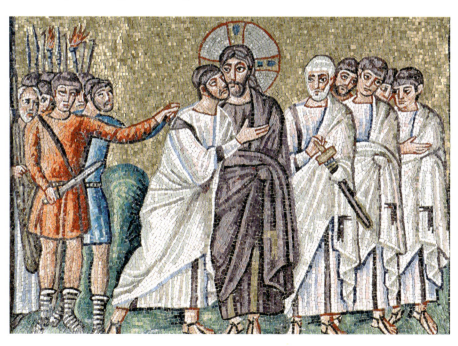

LATE 5ᵀᴴ EARLY 6ᵀᴴ CENTURY

ARCHIEPISCOPAL (ST. ANDREW'S) CHAPEL

HISTORICAL BACKGROUND

The Archiepiscopal Chapel, also known as Saint Andrew's Chapel, built as a private oratory for the Catholic bishops at the height of Theodoric's reign at the time of Bishop Peter II (494-519), is located on the first floor of the present-day bishop's palace and entrance is gained from the first room of the Archiepiscopal Museum.

Presumably it was originally dedicated to Christ who dominates every part of the mosaic decoration. For reasons of ecclesiastical politics it was later dedicated to Saint Andrew whose relics were transported by Maximian from Constantinople to Ravenna (middle of the 6th century). Substantial changes were made to the building in the 16th century and with substitution of some mosaics with frescoes by Luca Longhi. In the 17th century a new entrance was made in the apse area and in so doing the internal orientation was upset. In 1734 Archbishop Farsetti had a room built next to this chapel which is currently used as the Archiepiscopal Museum.

A restoration programme started in 1911 aimed at bringing the chapel back to its original state.

DESCRIPTION

The chapel, consisting of a square room with apse with four corner pillars that give it the form of a Greek cross, is covered by a cross vault and preceded by a rectangular vestibule with a barrel vault.

The entire building is in brick. Entry is gained through a door in the north side of the vestibule. The walls are completely decorated with marble in the lower part and mosaics in the upper part.

A lunette above the entrance door depicting a warrior Christ on a gold background (restored from the middle downward with fresco) dominates the vestibule. He is shown frontally wearing a cuirass, purple mantle and military style footwear with a cross resting on his right shoulder and the left hand holding an open book with the inscription *"Ego sum via, veritas et vita"* (John 14.6). He stands victoriously crushing a lion and a snake under his feet, the symbols of evil as expressed in a verse from psalm 91.13 *"super aspidem et basiliscum ambulabis et conculcabis leonem et draconem"*.

The vault is covered with an elegant decorative motif in tempera consisting of a network of white lilies and rosettes that create the effect of an airy pergola. The lozenge shaped spaces of the decorative grid contain various species of small birds such as doves, ducks, parrots and partridges, etc.

on a gold background evoking the peaceful atmosphere of heaven. Lower down a Latin inscription of twenty hexameters runs along the walls of the vestibule. This was completely redone in tempera in 1911 by Gerola on the basis of the original text quoted by the proto-historian Andreas Agnellus in his *Liber Pontificalis Ecclesiae Ravennatis*.

At the centre of the cross vault of the chapel a medallion bearing Christ's monogram is depicted. It is held up by four angels with upraised arms arranged on the ribs of the vault on a gold background.

The triangular spaces between the angels the winged symbols of the Evangelists holding their respective gospels emerge from colourful clouds.

At the top of the soffits of the arches supporting the vault there is either an image of Christ or disk with Christ's monogram and on either side a series of medallions containing images of apostles and saints. In the east and west arches Christ is flanked by the twelve apostles while in the north and south arches male and female saints.

The conch of the apse was completely redecorated with fresco at the beginning of the nineteen hundreds with a starry sky that resembles the one in Galla Placidia's Mausoleum.

Justification for inclusion in the World Heritage List

This chapel is the only example of a bishop's chapel that has come down to us intact. It is also the only orthodox monument built during the reign of Theodoric and the consequent predomination of the Arian religion. From the architectural viewpoint the chapel is quite similar to the Mausoleum of Galla Placidia and more generally to the type of cruciform buildings built in the 5th and 6th centuries in the northern Adriatic area and which are still extant at Verona (shrine of Saint Tosca and Saint Teuteria), Padua (St. Prosdocimus), Vicenza (shrine of Santa Maria Mater Domini), Pola (shrine of Santa Maria del Canneto).

Its mosaic decoration is of great interest as the themes represented can also be interpreted in an anti-Arian sense, bearing witness to the fact that at the height of Theodoric's reign, in spite of the peaceful coexistence of Latins and Goths, Orthodox and Arian, and the neutrality of the Gothic king, the Catholic bishops were deeply concerned about the new rulers and their Arian religion.

Taken as a whole the decorative plan of the chapel is clearly intended to glorify Christ, whose monogram and face are depicted a number of times and whose victorious figure appears on over the entrance door, a position that clearly alludes to Christ as the one who opens the gates of heaven. The images of martyrs, apostles and evangelists further underline this concept of glorification, which is expressed to the highest degree by the angels who, in the guise of winged victories, hold up the Christological monogram at the top of the cross vault.

Noteworthy from the iconological viewpoint is the figure of the warrior Christ – the only claimed example in early Christian art – having its origin in imperial art and more specifically in a fresco, which unfortunately has been lost, in the vestibule of the Imperial Palace in Constantinople where, according to the description by Eusebius, the emperor Constantine was depicted in the act of running a serpent through, a symbol of the vanquished enemy.

Nevertheless, the image of Christ crushing the lion and the serpent in the Archiepiscopal Chapel can be considered not only as a victory over the power of evil but more particularly as a victory over the heretics of the Arian religion. In this light the words inscribed in the open book *"Ego sum via, veritas et vita"* (I am the way, the truth and the life) take on a distinctly anti-Arian meaning as they reinforce the orthodox dogma concerning the human and divine nature of Christ and therefore the consubstantiality of Father and Son denied by the Arians.

As to the peculiarities of the mosaic decoration, the chapel contains the oldest examples that have come down to us of *imagines clipeatae*, the series of medallions containing the busts of Christ, the apostles and martyrs that was to become very common in mosaics of the 6th century as seen in the Basilica of San Vitale, the Monastery of Saint Catherine on Mount Sinai and the Euphrasian Basilica of Parenzo.

Another noteworthy feature in the chapel is that the medallions on the lower faces of the arches depicting twelve martyrs provide a clear affirmation of Catholic orthodoxy

Archiepiscopal Chapel

since the Arians did not practice any veneration of saints.

Finally, in the polemical spirit of anti-Arianism previously mentioned, the exaltation of light in the Latin inscription on the walls of the oratory "Aut Lux hic nata est aut capta hic libera regnat" (Either light was born here or, captured here reigns freely) can be interpreted in the same way.

These verses, which are usually believed to express in poetical form the brilliance of the light issuing from the thousands of mosaic tiles of Ravenna, can also be interpreted as a direct allusion to divine light and orthodoxy in particular.

LATE 5TH EARLY 6TH CENTURY

Theodoric's Mausoleum

Historical Background

This majestic and austere monument is located approximately one kilometre from the centre of Ravenna, beyond the ancient city walls and in an area used by the Goths as a graveyard. Theodoric (493-526) had it built while he was still alive according to the Anonymous Valesiano (546-552) and the protohistorian Andreas Agnellus (middle of the ninth century).

It was later dedicated to Saint Mary and used as a Christian oratory after Justinian's edict. During this period of anti-Arian fanaticism the porphyry sarcophagus containing the mortal remains of Theodoric was removed from the building and relocated many times.

A square tower was built next to the oratory and later used as a lighthouse from which it later took the new name of S. Maria *ad Pharum*. In the 12th century a Benedictine monastery was built alongside. In the Middle Ages the oratory was again used as a Mausoleum for the burial of important people such as Pope Victor II in 1057, Paolo Traversari in 1240, etc.

The following centuries saw the mausoleum in a state of complete abandonment, a fact eloquently revealed in various illustrations (one from the fifteen hundreds by an unknown artist and kept in Vienna and another by Vincenzo Coronelli of the 18th century which show the monument buried up to the springers of the lower floor arches. This was due mainly to the nearby River Badareno, a tributary of the Po, breaking its banks.

In 1748 attempts were made to reclaim the surrounding area which was completely swamped and in 1774 two staircases were built to the upper floor.

Then in 1844 the problem of drainage and excavation of the area around the mausoleum was effectively resolved.

The eighteenth century staircases were removed in 1918 and in 1927 the present metal walkway was installed.

In 1977 restoration work was done under the direction of the Superintendency for Environmental and Architectural Heritage of Ravenna in which the surrounding area was landscaped and the floors of the two levels were restored.

DESCRIPTION

The walls of this austere and impressive mausoleum sink about 2 metres below ground level and rest on a foundation bed of conglomerate of whole and fragmented bricks, stones and lime about 1.5 metres thick which would have given the building stability.

Originally the building was surrounded by ten pillars, some of which were discovered in the foundations during archaeological excavations or in ancient drawings, all connected by metal railings.

Compared to all the other buildings of Ravenna, which are of brick, the mausoleum is unusual for its walls of Istrian stone blocks. In construction the Istrian stone was cut precisely into regular blocks which were laid using a dry technique without mortar and connected with dovetailed iron cramps.

The blocks were worked with great precision and a groove cut along the edges accentuates their regularity. This can be seen also in the arches, constructed using stone quoins with interlocking teeth joined using scarf joints and a keystone at the centre of the vault.

The mausoleum consists of two superimposed levels. The lower level is decagonal and on each side there is a rectangular niche with a round arch above. The entrance to the lower level is located in the niche on the western side leading to a cruciform chamber with a cross vault lit by six small widows and originally used for religious services.

The upper level, smaller by about 1.3 m is also decagonal up to the height of the entrance door after which it becomes circular, perhaps to facilitate placing the great monolithic cupola. This circular band, which contains eleven windows (some with one light and some with two), is delimited at the top and bottom by two high cornices, the upper of which is decorated with a style called "pincer frieze" which can also be seen in gothic gold.

In the decagonal part there are signs of unfinished work; in fact each side has two rectangular niches above which blind lunettes jut out while at the corners of the building there are columns with pyramidal projections at the top. Various suggestions have been made as to how the structure would have been completed. One idea hypothesises an external gallery with columns with protruding niches containing statues and small arches. However on the basis of the decorative elements which were widespread at Theodoric's time, it is possible to hypothesise a large scalloped niche in the lunettes, subdivided by corbels with small winged victories, features which can be seen in the drawings of a hypothetical completion by Heidenreich and Johannes.

A rectangular door on the western side, heavily outlined by cornices, gives access to the upper level which has a circular plan of radius 9.2 m and which was to be the funeral chamber still containing the porphyry sarcophagus which would have contained the mortal remains of the Gothic king and which was returned here only in 1913 after numerous relocations and vicissitudes.

The upper level is capped by the great monolithic dome, which is the distinguishing feature of this building, crowned with twelve loops bearing the names of eight apostles

Theodoric's Mausoleum

and the four evangelists. The *ingens saxum* mentioned by Anonymous Valesiano measures 10.76 m in diameter and 3.09 m in height and weights 230 tons according to recent calculations.

A disc of diameter 3.75 m on the extrados of the dome protrudes 10 cm with a parallelepiped element at the centre on which a metal cross stands.

There is also a large fissure in the monolith, probably caused by difficult work of raising and placing whereas – according to popular legend – the dome was split by a lightening bolt during a storm which struck Theodoric, who had taken refuge inside, and reduced him to ashes for his crimes.

JUSTIFICATION FOR INCLUSION IN THE WORLD HERITAGE LIST

In no other location of late antiquity has a tomb of this type come down to us.

The uniqueness of Theodoric's Mausoleum, the tomb of the King of the Ostrogoths, lies in its architecture which is without parallel in the construction methods of the Roman, late antiquity or Byzantine periods. In a new original way it amalgamates elements and ideas from different architectural and artistic traditions: Roman, Syrian, Constantinopolitan, and finally barbarian.

As regards materials, the use of Istrian stone instead of brick distinguishes it from all the other buildings not only in Ravenna but from all Byzantine and early Christian architecture in the West in general.

Construction using blocks of stone is typical of Syria, Palestine and a great part of Asia Minor which have an abundance of this construction material and it is precisely from these regions that the highly specialised craftsmen who built the tomb, using a perfect system of dry connection of rigorously squared and finished blocks, came. Every block was planned, cut and finely worked in order to achieve the most effective solution for stability of the building.

While the use of large stone blocks lent itself admirably to the construction of vertical surfaces, this was not the case for roofing which, in the near East, was a method employed only to cover small spaces. For the roofing of larger spaces wood or brick were used. No historical records exist referring to the use of a monolith of such extraordinary size as that of Theodoric's Mausoleum. The shallow monolithic cupola seems to be an interpretation of the Byzantine brick cupolas which Theodoric must have been very familiar with when living at the court of Constantinople as the adoptive son of the emperor Zeno.

In fact we know that this choice was made at the express will of Theodoric who, according to Anonymous Valesiano, *"se autem vivo fecit sibi monumentum ex lapide quadrato mirae magnitudinis opus, et saxum ingentem quem superponeret inquisivit"* (While still alive he built for himself a funerary monument in squared stone of marvellous size had his servants search for a huge mass to cover it).

For this reason many experts have attributed a meaning to it that goes beyond constructional considerations giving it a purely celebrative character and seeing it as a symbol of power.

A number of highly varied symbolic interpretations have been put forward regarding this unusual roof. Some experts maintain that it recalls the great megalithic tombs of Nordic countries or it could be a translation into stone of the tents of the ancient Goths (in this case the twelve sides would represent the metal poles used to support the tent).

For other experts this roof could suggest the idea of a royal crown or a warrior's helmet or even the dome of the sky.

Of the many hypotheses, there is one of particular interest in which Theodoric placed his sarcophagus under a cupola surrounded by twelve sides with the names of the apostles in order to evoke Constantine's tomb in the imperial mausoleum of Constantinople in which the emperor's tomb was surrounded

Theodoric's Mausoleum

by cenotaphs of the twelve apostles.

Aside from the symbolic interpretations that give particular importance to the monument, it should be noted that even today what is of great interest to experts concerns the transport and placement of the monolith and the related technical problems. If it had to be transported by sea from the cost of Istria to that of Ravenna the operations of raising it to the top of the building were even more complex. It is likely that it was raised using a slope and moved upward using rollers, a hypothesis advanced by most experts, alternatively it could have been lifted using a platform of large trunks.

Another unique feature is its architectural form consisting of the superimposition of one level above another, the lower of which

Theodoric's Mausoleum

Theodoric's Mausoleum

is decagonal and the upper level narrower and changing from decagonal to circular.

The problem now arises of the influences incorporated in such an unusual monument full of heterogeneous components. The distinctly Roman style of the lower level with its deep arches and the "gothic" style of the decorations in the second level, especially in the motives of the frieze, have led to the hypothesis of two architects, one of western, Roman origin who designed the entire building who for reasons unknown was replaced by a gothic architect who would have partially changed the original design giving the top of the mausoleum a circular form.

While it is true that this type of imperial mausoleum with two levels was particularly widespread in Rome and Gaul, the most similar examples are without doubt to be found in Syria in the 5th and 6th centuries and it is precisely in Syria, with its abundant supplies of stone, that they use the same type of construction materials in square blocks with ornate cornices exactly as we find in our mausoleum.

Recently these considerations have led experts to suggest that this mausoleum was built by foreign labour, probably from Isauria, brought to Ravenna especially to build the mausoleum which was to be distinctive from all others and at the same time testify to the eclectic politics of the gothic king Theodoric.

The uniqueness of this monument which, as we have seen, also poses problems of an architectural, historic, artistic and semantic nature is also confirmed by the interest awakened in the artists and architects of the past.

Apart from a drawing kept in the Hofbibliotek of Vienna by an anonymous Italian author of the 16th century, two drawings by the famous architect Giuliano da Sangallo (1443-15169) are known, one of which is a part of his "Book of Roman sketches" and the other is kept in the Uffizi Gallery of Florence. There are also various prints by Giovanni Battista Piranesi (1744), Vincenzo Coronelli (1708) and Pietro Santi (1760) which depict the monument buried in the ground up to the arches of the lower level. In the field of painting the mausoleum appears in the "Transfiguration of Christ" by Giovanni Bellini (1430-1516) now at the National Gallery of Capodimonte in Naples and in a painting by Marco Palmezzano (1459-1539) depicting the "Pietà" and kept in the sacristy of the Cathedral of Ravenna.

The Mausoleum of the gothic king thus became one of the main attractions for travellers of the nineteenth century "Grand Tour" who were fascinated by Ravenna and its art treasures.

6TH CENTURY

Basilica of San Vitale

Historical Background

The earliest historical information we have about this church is to be found in the *Liber Pontificalis Ecclesiae Ravennatis* of Andreas Agnellus who, during the lifetime of Maximian, quotes an epigraph which was located in the narthex of the church with the following text:

"Beatis Martiris Vitalis Basilica mandante Eclesio vero (=viro) beatissimo Episcopo a fundamentis Iulianus Argentarius edificavit ornavit atque dedicavit consecrante vero reverendissimo Maximiano episcopo sud die XVI Kal. Iunii indictione X septies p.c. Pacifici Basilii iunioris V C."

This inscription can be considered a genuine legal document as we are able to deduce from it that:

1) The bishop was the *episcopus mandans*, in other words the commissioner of the works; it was he who ordered the building of the church after his return from Constantinople together with Pope John in AD 525. It is quite probable that work began around the year 526 after the death of Theodoric when Amalasuntha, regent and governor of Theodoric's son Athalaric showed herself to be well-disposed toward the Catholics;
2) Construction was entrusted to Julianus Argentarius;
3) It was consecrated by Maximian in 547

The church was built on a 5th century temple in memory of the martyr Vitale which was to be incorporated into the building.
According to a legend originating probably in the 6th century and intending to ennoble the origins of the church, the site on which it was built is where San Vitale was martyred. In reality we know that the body of this saint, together with that of Agricola, was found in Bologna by St. Ambrose in 393.
The front of the church originally had a

Basilica of San Vitale

quadrangular porch, discovered by Maioli at the beginning of the 20th century, and later replaced with a Benedictine cloister at some time during the tenth century.

It was perhaps in this period that the cupola was decorated with Byzantine style frescoes and the bell tower was built on the staired tower to the right of the narthex which, together with the staircase on the left, led to the matroneum.

The present-day bell tower dates from 1696 when it was partially rebuilt in the same century after an earthquake.

In the 16th century the old cloister was replaced with a Renaissance cloister by Andrea Della Valle and the flooring of the church was raised by 80 cm to avoid seepage from the water table due to subsidence and covered with polychrome marble (1538-1545).

The cupola was frescoed once again by Bertuzzi and Tonduzzi who were artists from Faenza. Then between 1778 and 1782 it was covered with a new series of frescoes in baroque style by the artists Barozzi, Gandolfi and Guarana.

Between the late 19th and early 20th centuries substantial restoration work was done under Corradi Ricci, renovating the northern stair tower and the marble covering of the apse and presbytery modelled on the example of the Euphrasian Basilica at Parenzo (Istria). The choir floor was also raised by about 50 cm at this time.

Restoration work has also been done recently by the Superintendency for Environmental and Architectural Heritage of Ravenna.

Description

San Vitale is without doubt one of Ravenna's most impressive historic buildings. The church is on an octagonal plan and constructed in long flat bricks (4 x 48 cm) joined with thick layers of lime of the same thickness, a type of brickwork typical of all the buildings constructed by Julianus Argentarius. The structure divides into two octagonal prismatic bodies of which the lower is larger and the upper is narrower encircling the cupola.

At the centre of each side of the upper level a wide arch encloses a window. The lower part has two rows of windows separated by a narrow crenelled cornice. Each of the lower side walls is delineated by two pilasters that reach to the eaves of the roof while strong buttresses rise up at the corners ending in triangular tympani.

The apse on the eastern side, internally semi-circular and externally polygonal, is flanked by two small rectangular rooms ending in niches and semicircular sacristies, a *diaconicon* and a *prothesis* with rectangular additions.

On the opposite side there is the original imposing entrance consisting of an unusual forceps-shaped narthex ending in two exedrae opposite each other and which was originally preceded by a quadrangular porch. This narthex is arranged asymmetrically with respect to the building's main axis. In fact it is not connected to the side of the octagon opposite the apse but rests against one of the corners. This arrangement produces two triangular rooms at the ends of which the staired towers stand giving access to the matroneum.

The internal architecture of San Vitale creates a space that expands in all directions; it stretches out around us in the exedrae and upward to the high cupola. The succes-

Basilica of San Vitale

sion of full and empty spaces, the rhythmic play of the arches with the eight pilasters sheathed with veined marble, the contrast between the light filtering down from the windows of the tambour and the gloom that envelops the ambulatory and the matroneum creates an evocative atmosphere. On the eastern side stands the presbytery area ending in a semi-round apse.

The cupola, which stands on eight pilasters with a diameter of 16 metres is one of the church's most important architectural features. It consists of horizontal concentric rings of twin terracotta pipes superimposed in diminishing diameters. This material makes it possible to build upward without requiring great thickness in the side walls (those of San Vitale measure only 0.95 m). It is now decorated with baroque frescoes in strong contrast to the purity of the architectural lines of the church. Never at any point in its history has it been decorated with mosaics.

Also worthy of note are the columns and capitals of the exedrae and the triforia. The columns are tall and elegant, probably imported from the East. Those of the ground floor rest on octagonal bases and are surmounted by refined impost-capitals in the form of lotus leaves having the form of truncated inverted pyramids thus connecting easily the circular shape of the column to the square shape of the vaulting.

Similar capitals, with abstract decorative motifs in a compressed bas-relief can be found in Constantinople. It is almost certain that they were imported from the eastern capital since it is at Byzantium at the beginning of

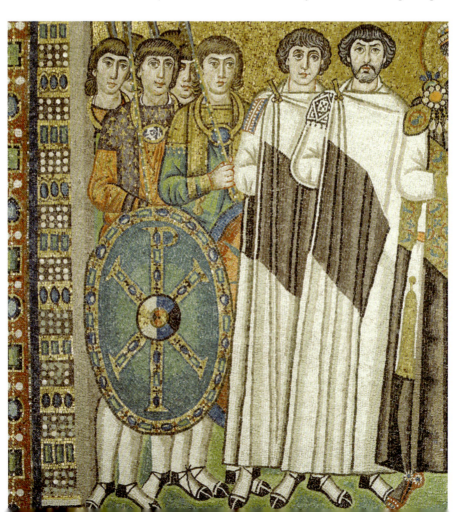

BASILICA OF SAN VITALE

the 6th century that the impost-capital was invented replacing almost everywhere the Corinthian and composite types.

Other types of impost-capitals, particularly refined, are to be found in San Vitale. In the southern triforium of the presbytery they are adorned with a border of laurel leaves and a stylised plant motif of great refinement on all four faces. The faces of the lower triforia are decorated with plant motifs of acanthus leaves which come together to form orbs and are interwoven to form a cross giving the effect of a rich lacework in marble.

Another variation on the impost-capital theme is to be found in the northern triforium of the presbytery, at the level of the matroneum; at the corners and in the middle they have cusps, the capital as a whole giving the idea of an exquisitely worked marble basket. Similar examples can be found in the Church of St. Sergius and St. Bacchus in Constantinople and in the Church of St. Demetrius in Thessalonika.

Of the eight sections which make up the present flooring, six are datable to the Renaissance period and are of marble inlay while the remaining two are of the 6th century.

The two original sections in mosaic have almost identical decoration: at the centre of the base of the triangle there is a cantharus (vase) out of which plant fronds flow and fill the surface with their convolutions which envelop small birds and bunches of grapes.

The richness and sumptuousness of the church would have been heightened by the marble facing which originally covered all the lower walls. Also worthy of note is the 6th century stucco decoration on the intrados of the arches in the presbytery and which still retains traces of the original colouring.

Entry into the presbytery is through large arch with a wide intrados decorated with fifteen medallions containing busts of Christ (at the top), the twelve apostles and presumed figures of San Vitale, St. Gervase and St. Protasius at the sides.

The cross vaulting is divided into four triangles by four festoons of leaves and fruit which converge toward a garland encircling the mystic lamb, held by four angels surrounded by spirals of acanthus coloured green with highlights in gold or gold with highlights in green. Every triangle is a profusion of flowers stars, birds and animals of various species.

In the presbytery there are triforia on the ground floor level and the level above with refined columns and openwork capitals. The

Basilica of San Vitale

walls are decorated with mosaics depicting scenes from the Old Testament (lower level) and New Testament (upper level).

On the left in a large lunette there are episodes from the life of Abraham: first the patriarch offers hospitality to the three angels, seated at a table in the centre, who had come to announce the birth of a son to him and his wife Sara, then on the right he is stopped by a divine hand before the sacrifice of his son Isaac in whose place a ram is sacrificed. His wife Sara, visible at the threshold of the hut, has a smile on her lips as she listens to the announcement of her imminent motherhood. The biblical scene is told in all its details with great realism.

Above the lunette two angels are depicted in flight and holding a disc containing a cross. On the left the prophet Jeremiah is represented holding a scroll and on the right two scenes concerning Moses: Moses receives the tablets of the law from the hand of God while below the people of Israel wait for his return at the foot of the holy mountain on which they are not permitted to set foot. At the sides of the upper triforium the two evangelists John and Luke surmounted by their symbols (the eagle and calf) are represented.

The decoration on the right wall of the presbytery corresponds perfectly in its compositional make-up; two Old Testament scenes are depicted in a lunette in the lower level, the sacrifices of Abel and Melchisedek. Abel, placed next to a lowly hut and wearing a short animal skin, offers a lamb to God whose hand emerges from a cloud to confer a blessing. On the right the great priest Melchizedek wearing magnificent robes and with a sumptuous temple in the background offers a paten to God. Between them stands an altar covered with a beautiful white cloth on which the symbols of the Eucharist, a chalice and bread, have been placed. Above the lunette there are gain two angels in flight and holding a disc containing a cross. On the right the prophet Isaiah and on the left two more scenes from the life of Moses are represented. Moses watches over the flock of his father-in-law Jethro and in the next scene he unlatches his shoes before approaching the burning bush.

To the sides of the upper triforium the other two evangelists Matthew and Mark are represented surmounted respectively by their symbols (the man and the winged lion). On the sides of the extrados of the triumphal arch the two cities of Jerusalem and Bethlehem are depicted symbolising respectively the Church of the Jews and the Church of the Gentiles. At the centre two angels poised in flight hold a medallion containing a monogram of Christ with eight rays and the letter alpha at the centre. Above the arch a triforium opens surrounded by an elegant mosaic decoration of vine garlands.

In the vault of the apse, above the three great windows, a veritable theophany is depicted: Christ stands out in all his glory on a gold background, seated on a blue globe,

BASILICA OF SAN VITALE

dressed in purple edged with gold stripes and flanked by two archangels. In his left hand he holds the scroll of the seven seals and in the right hand a triumphal crown which he offers to Vitale, the patron saint of the church depicted on the left. On the opposite side Bishop Ecclesius offers the model of the church of San Vitale which he commissioned.

At the foot of the apse side walls are the famous panels depicting the Emperor Justinian and the Empress Theodora while offering a gift of sacred vessels to the church on the occasion of its consecration.

On the left wall the emperor, dressed in purple and holding a large gold paten is surrounded by other court dignitaries followed by a group of guards of honour and preceded by religious personages, one of whom is the bishop Maximian who stands out from the others and is identified by an inscription located above his head. Between him and the emperor stands another person with distinct facial features for whom many identities have been suggested. This could be Julianus Argentarius, the banker-financier of the church or the possibly the prefect of the praetorium, a high imperial functionary residing in Ravenna.

In the panel on the right wall the Empress Theodora is the undisputed dominant figure. She is depicted advancing and holding a gold chalice adorned with precious stones. She is preceded by two dignitaries and accompanied by a group of ladies-in-waiting from whom she is distinguished by the purple garments and the great diadem, precious stones and pearls that adorn her haloed head. The atmosphere of luxury and splendour, which must have typified the court of Byzantium, is also suggested by the multicoloured drapes and magnificent garments rich in colours and decorative motifs worn by the ladies-in-waiting.

Justification for inclusion
in the World Heritage List

The Basilica of San Vitale is a unique example of Byzantine art; firstly because it blends in a most original way eastern and western styles into its architecture and secondly because its well-conserved mosaics clearly express the ideology and religiosity of the Justinian era which has been defined as the First golden Age of Byzantine Art.

If in the east, the Church of St. Sophia of Constantinople (532-537) is considered the great masterpiece of Byzantine art, the Basilica of San Vitale has been defined as "the only truly extraordinary building of the 6th century in the West".

Unlike St. Sophia which underwent numerous remodelling works both during the Justinian era and after the arrival of the Turks (4453), the church of San Vitale has remained substantially unchanged and therefore it retains the original spaces and mosaic decorations.

As an expression of official Justinian art it was taken as a model for the Carolingian chapel of Aachen.

For such an exceptional building the *regio Domus Augustae*, an area full of luxury Roman residences and imperial buildings such as the church of Santa Croce with the famous annexed mausoleum commissioned by Galla Placidia, was chosen.

This quarter was also characterised by the presence of other sacred buildings such as Santa Maria Maggiore, built between 526 and 532 at the same time as the initial construction phase of San Vitale, and Santo Stefano Maggiore which was commissioned by Maximian.

San Vitale is clearly different from these two buildings with its clear central plan and its well articulated architecture which seems to reveal an imperial purpose even if the emperor in person never came to Ravenna. This would explain why the upper colonnade, intended to host the imperial gallery in the part in front of the presbytery was left unfinished.

This building also expressed well the political and religious intent of Justinian through its architecture based on a central plan and the mosaic decorations, demonstrating how art

can become *instrumentum regni*.

In regard to the octagonal plan with double shell, a distant precedent can be found in the Golden Octagon of Antioch (327-341), a church annexed to the imperial palace of Constantine. A nearby example from Justinian times is the Church of St. Sergius and St. Bacchus in Constantinople. This was one of the first worship buildings commissioned by Justinian between 527 and 536 and from which San Vitale is different due to its unusual architectural features and above all for its simple clear plan, interrupted on the eastern side by a particularly complex and articulated apse. Here the various heights of the apse and the circular pastophoria with rectangular annexes create the impression of a refined play of volumes full of chiaroscuro effects and vertical movement. This is also evident in the area of the narthex, flanked by the two staired towers. In addition, the unusual position of the narthex, which rests against a corner instead of the side opposite the apse and therefore located asymmetrically with respect to the main axis of the church, has no parallels in other buildings built before or after and often suggesting contrasting hypotheses to the experts.

It is however probable that this solution was imposed by the need to obtain greater space for access to the church by means of an entrance through two adjacent sides, at the same time leaving space for the staired towers.

Another unusual feature in the sphere of western religious construction is the presence of the gallery in the upper storey, known as the matroneum or gynaeceum as it was destined for use by women while the men remained on the ground floor. What distinguishes San Vitale more than anything from all other Byzantine churches is its particular arrangement of internal spaces with their upward thrust.

The internal architecture, in perfect accord with the mosaic and sculpted decoration, creates a seemingly unlimited space which expands in all directions into the empty exedrae, spreading out like the crown of a flower and soaring up into the great round of the cupola.

The close alternation of empty and full spaces, the rhythmic play of the arches, the scenic perspective of the ambulatory in shadowy contrast to the luminous central space produce an effect of virtual existence while the strong vertical rhythm and the restlessness of the lower levels are resolved in a dynamic upward thrust.

This dominating verticality is a hallmark of San Vitale and distinguishes it from contemporary Justinian buildings such as St. Sophia and St. Sergius and St. Bacchus of Constantinople where the space seems to extend to infinity but is limited by the low brick cupola.

The architect of San Vitale, most probably from the west, therefore translated in original terms the new Justinian architecture, combining elements of oriental origin (the

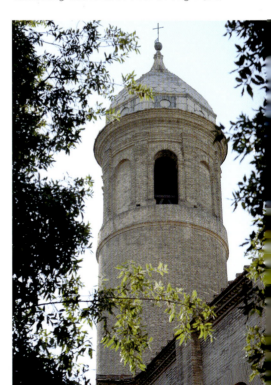

Basilica of San Vitale

octagonal plan, the type of walls, the apse with polygonal external wall and semicircular internal wall, the pastophoria, the matroneum, the columns, the capitals and the dosserets) with other features of western origin (the forceps-shaped narthex, the staired towers, the tambour, the constructional technique of the cupola in clay piping and the system of round arches, the use of pilaster strips and buttresses).

It was with good reason therefore that Ravenna's first historian Andreas Agnellus wrote these words in reference to San Vitale: *"Nulla in Italia ecclesia similes est in aedificiis et in mecanicis operibus"* (No church in Italy can be considered similar to San Vitale for audacity of structure and technical know-how).

As mentioned above, the exceptional architectural characteristics of San Vitale was the reason for its choice by Charlemagne as the model for his palatine chapel in Aachen which, consecrated in 805, can be considered the most important building with a central plan of the Carolingian period.

Charlemagne's chapel is octagonal with a gallery in the upper level and surmounted by a cupola in which the overall effect however is different, appearing weightier and without that sense of lightness and airiness that characterises San Vitale.

The link with San Vitale, besides being formal is above all spiritual: At the time of Charlemagne the splendour of Ravenna as the last capital of the empire in the west had not yet been extinguished. For this reason Charlemagne not only brought marble columns, paving stones and the equine statue of Theodoric but to connect himself more with its glorious past – thus legitimising also his power – he drew inspiration from San Vitale for the architectural design of his chapel.

Much later in the Renaissance the architecture of San Vitale attracted the attention of numerous artists. Filippo Brunelleschi was inspired by it while working on plans for the Rotonda di Santa Maria degli Angeli (1434-1436) in Florence, the construction of which unfortunately was never finished. In the frescoes in the Zodiac Room of the Palace of Mantua, painted between 1525 and 1530, there appear views of Theodoric's tomb, the Port'Aurea, the outside of San Vitale and the inside converted into a temple to Neptune.

Basilica of San Vitale

Just as in the Mausoleum of Galla Placidia the architecture and decoration are inextricably combined, the same is true of San Vitale which is unthinkable without the rich mosaics which, being brought to life by the light, transfigure the architectural organism.

The mosaics, which should be considered an integral part of the architecture, seem to enclose the congregation in an atmosphere that is both magical and beautiful, a symphony of shapes and symbols capable of inspiring the soul and lifting it toward the divine realm.

To imagine the effect on the believers entering a Byzantine church such as San Vitale we can borrow a description of the interior of St. Sophia given by Procopius: "On entering the church to pray one immediately feels that this is not the work of man but rather the work of a divine power; and the spirit, in its ascent toward the sky senses the presence of God and that He delights in this dwelling that he has chosen for Himself".

In fact we have to imagine San Vitale in its original state which was then much more opulent not only with its wall mosaics of which some have a gold background, but also a mosaic floor, marble wall covering and polychrome stuccos under the arches and vaults. If we add to this sumptuous decoration silk drapes and materials, gold and silver liturgical vessels studded with gems and candelabras in other precious metals that once adorned the church, it is possible to imagine the dazzling atmosphere inside such a place of worship, capable of elevating the souls of the believers and transporting them into an unearthly dimension.

In regard to the wall mosaics, several expressive languages can be identified.

While the mosaics of the presbytery the figures have diverse postures, represented in profile or three-quarters view and placed on a landscape background, in the area of the apse the figures are represented only in frontal view, appearing flat against the background, linear and hieratic. Without any connection with earthly reality they stand on a gold background, abstract and unreal, giving them a metaphysical and transcendental character.

These differences were considered the result of different artistic periods or traditions.

Basilica of San Vitale

However, such diversity is not due to the fact that artists trained in the western tradition worked in the presbytery and those of Byzantine tradition in the apse, but rather to the need to express different concepts. To express the more "human" events of the Old Testament it was necessary to use a simpler, more natural and expressive language and characterised by a landscape background. To celebrate the divine and imperial world (Christ *cosmocratore* and the emperor representing God on earth) the language becomes more hieratic and abstract and the rigid frontally viewed personages are placed on a golden transcendental background.

These mosaics include the two famous panels of Justinian and Theodora, where the *augusti imperatori* appear in all their majesty and splendour. They represent not only examples of the highest form of Byzantine art but are absolutely unique and they enable us to form an idea of profane art at the court of Byzantium where it played an important role alongside religious art. These mosaic panels together with those of Emperor Constantine IV in Sant'Apollinare in Classe (7th century) are the oldest examples of historical-political panels that have come down to us.

Particularly worthy of note in the panel of Justinian are the extraordinary portraits Maximian and the presumed Julianus Argentarius (or possible the praetorian prefect) on the left of the emperor.

In the panel of Theodora, dominated by the personality of the august empress, two ladies-in-waiting have extremely well-defined facial features and to explain this it has been suggested that they represent Antonina and Giovannina, the wife and daughter respectively of Belisarius, the general who led the Byzantines in the conquest of Ravenna, while the other ladies-in-waiting, with rather stereotypical faces and beautiful garments and jewels contribute to conveying the idea of the opulence of the Byzantine court.

The two panels depict the offering of liturgical gifts to the church of San Vitale on the occasion of its consecration and the symbolic participation of the imperial couple in this ceremony at which they were not present however.

The imperial processions seem to be depicted before their entry into the church, perhaps in the narthex, as demonstrated by some architectural features and the fountain issuing water in the panel of Theodora and the diadem on the head of Justinian which would have been removed if he were actually inside the church.

The iconographic programme of San Vitale demonstrates great coherence and unity, exalting the salvation of humanity made possible by the sacrifice of Christ who is represented by the mystic lamb and prefigured by the Old Testament sacrifices of Isaac, Abel and Melchisedek. The episodes of the life of Moses also prefigure Christ and the divine law. Thus there is a perfect fusion of the Old and New Testaments which dominates the upper parts of the church, disseminated by the four evangelists and triumphant in the conch of the apse through the theophany of Christ cosmocrator seated on a blue globe and wearing purple robes. Below the celestial kingdom stand the earthly sovereigns Justinian and Theodora with their courtly entourages

The great importance given to the figure of the bishop Maximian, depicted next to the emperor, testifies to the perfect unity of Church and State achieved in this period. Elected as bishop by Justinian, Maximian always fell in line with imperial directives and, in recompense for his valuable political and religious work aimed at consolidating Byzantine rule in Italy; he was appointed archbishop becoming a kind of deputy of Papal authority.

Besides the political message, these mosaics express concepts that are rigidly orthodox, reinforcing the dogma of the trinity and the natural and divine nature of Christ in open contrast with Arian dogma and in defence of orthodox religion in the name of which the empire was reconquered.

The dogma of the trinity is expressed clearly by three angels depicted around a table in the lunette of Abraham and also by the numerous Christological monograms and crosses within three circles of different colours. One of these has the form of a radiant sun and after the Council of Nicaea it became widespread to give greater clarification to the consubstantiality of the Father, Son and Holy Spirit. The sun symbolised the Father, the rays the son and the heat the Holy Spirit.

The divine nature of Christ is then emphasised by the depiction of Christ cosmocrator (meaning Lord of the universe), much in the same way as God the Father dominating the apse and holding the scroll of the seven seals which only the mystic lamb can open. This apocalyptic image, together with that of sacrificial lamb at the centre of the vault of the presbytery, is intended to exalt the return of Christ in the Second Coming and therefore also his divine power.

The mosaics of San Vitale are without doubt a clear example of how art expresses the ideology of an age and the triumph of orthodoxy at the time of Justinian in a period when defenders of the Catholic faith often crossed swords with Monophysites and Arians over Christological disputes. They offer a pictorial commentary of the works of St. Ambrose who was one of the most active opposers of Arianism in the western Church.

6th Century

Basilica of Sant'Apollinare in Classe

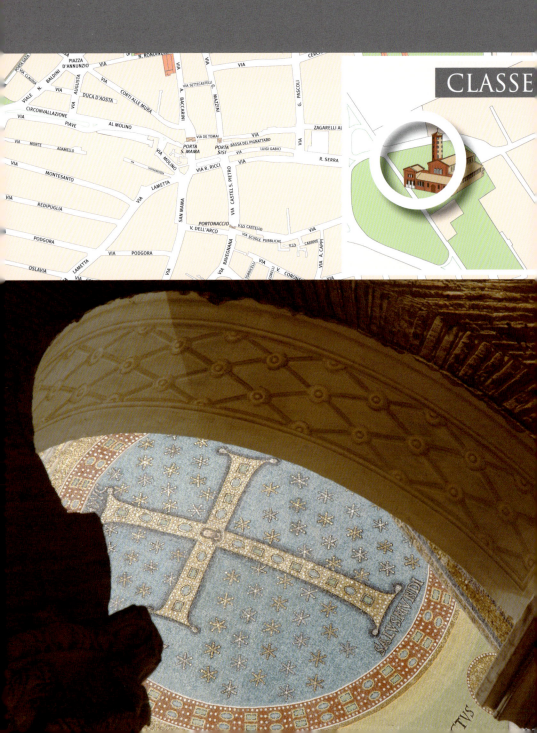

Historical Background

The Basilica of Sant'Apollinare in Classe rises in all its solemn grandeur about 8 km from the centre of Ravenna. The earliest historical reference we have to it comes from the historian Andreas Agnellus who, in his *Liber Pontificalis* in the biography of Maximian, records the text of a dedicatory epigraph – now lost – which was in the narthex of the basilica and which read as follows: *"Beati Apolenaris sacerdotis basilica(m) mandante vero (=viro) beatissimo Ursicino Episcopo a fundamentis Julianus Argentarius edificavit ornavit atque dedicavit consecrante vero (=viro) beato Maximiano Episcopo die VIIII Maiarum indicione XII octies Paci(fici Basilii =octies p.c. Basilii V.C.)"*

From this inscription we can deduce that the basilica was built at the time of the bishop Ursicinus who commissioned the building; that the "edificator ornator atque dedicator" was Julianus Argentarius and that the bishop who consecrated it was Maximian. The consecration took place on 9 May of the eighth year after the consulship of Basilisius and therefore in AD 549.

The historian Agnellus adds that no other church in Italy could compare with it for the beauty of the marbles that sparkled even at night.

In the second half of the 7th century, at the time of Archbishop Reparatus (671-677), important restoration work was done on the mosaics of the triumphal arch and the apse conch. During the 9th century further substantial restoration work was done on the roof, the mosaics of the triumphal arch and the quadrangular porch. In the same century the annular crypt was probably built under the presbytery and between the 10th and 11th centuries the great bell tower was most likely built.

At the beginning of the 12th century the mosaics on the pedestals of the triumphal arch (figures of the apostles) were replaced. In 1138 the Monastery of Classe passed from the Benedictine to the Camaldolensian order. In 1450 Sigismondo Pandolfo, from a noble family of Rimini, was responsible for ordering all the precious marble linings to be removed from the church.

The years 1723 to 1725 saw substantial work done in the presbytery area while the two stairways connecting the crypt to the presbytery were reduced to one only. Between 1776 and 1778 the portraits of the archbishops and bishops of Ravenna were painted in decorative medallions; the remaining ones can still be seen in the central nave above the arches.

Substantial restoration work, including the rebuilding of the narthex, was carried out under Corrado Ricci between 1897 and 1906.

In the 20th century numerous restoration works were done under the guidance of the Superintendency for Environmental and Architectural Heritage of Ravenna.

Description

The Basilica of Sant'Apollinare in Classe rises in all its solemn grandeur on a plan of 55.58 m length and 30.30 m width. The narthex is incorporated into the central body of its façade, framed by two pilasters, and ends in a quadrangular room with its own upper floor (small tower) which had its counterpart at the opposite end long since lost but of which the foundations have been unearthed. The external appearance of the basilica is therefore rather unbalanced. Towers such as these should be considered as originating from the eastern area of the empire, more specifically from Asia Minor.

The basilica originally must have appeared even more grandiose, since there was a quadrangular porch which extended out from the narthex and according to recent discoveries was wider than the basilica as it extended over the two northern and southern rooms (an expanded 'quadriportico').

The basilica, built out of so-called "Julian bricks" (each about 4 x 48 cm, divided by a layer of mortar of equal thickness), was constructed on an old burial ground in use from the late 2nd or early 3rd centuries until the period in which the basilica was built (middle of the 6th century).

This burial ground also contained the final resting place of the first bishop, Apollinaris, in a niche discovered about half-way along the southern side, outside the basilica. Opposite this point, on the wall of the church there is an epigraph, believed to date from the middle of the 6th century, stating that the burial urn of St. Apollinaris was transferred inside the basilica at the time of Maximian (+ in hoc loco stetit arca beati Apolenaris sacerdotis et confessoris…).

From the outside the basilica appears as a simple neat involucrum, entirely in elegant brickwork. The interior is characterised by spaciousness which suggests an abstract transcendental dimension, imposing in its grandeur and magnificence. It is divided into three naves, of which the central nave is twice the width of the other two, and two rows of twelve columns of beautiful Greek marble from the Sea of Marmara (Andreas Agnellus), resting on cube-like bases decorated with a lozenge motif, something very common in Constantinople and the eastern world generally.

Also worthy of note are the refined capitals described as "acanthus leaves stirred by the wind" or "butterfly-form" on account of the impression they give: the acanthus leaves are in fact flowing as if raised by the wind and being in opposing pairs suggest the effect of butterfly wings. This leaves have been worked minutely with a drill creating colouristic and chiaroscuro effects: rows of flowers bring out the lines of the

Basilica of Sant'Apollinare in Classe

leaves. Similar capitals are known in Greece and Constantinople.

Between the arches along the central nave there is a series of medallions containing cameo portraits of the bishops and archbishops of Ravenna frescoed in the 18th century.

The church would have been much more sumptuous with its mosaic floor decorated with geometric motifs and of which remains have been found at the end of the left nave, at the centre of the middle nave and at the beginning of the right nave. In the last mentioned there is an inscription which reads "Gaudentia" and "Felix", the names of two benefactors of the church who contributed financially to the construction of the floor. These mosaics were discovered at only 30-35 cm depth since the basilica, unlike many other buildings of Ravenna, has not been elevated to the point of altering its vertical proportions.

The opulence of the interior must have been enhanced by the precious marbles that dressed its side walls, removed by Sigismondo Pandolfo Malatesta in the first half of the fourteen hundreds to adorn the temple he had commissioned in Rimini. Originally there were three doors in the side walls.

The basilica ends with an apse semicircular inside and polygonal outside flanked by two square rooms ending in a small polygonal apse (*pastophorium*), an oriental custom but which became a tradition of Ravenna.

The presbytery of the church is now considerably raised (1.88 m) above floor level, the result of an alteration to accommodate the building of a crypt.

The presbytery area was originally occupied by the 'bema', a square space reserved for the clergy and closed off by plutei and transepts, the foundations of which were un-

Basilica of Sant'Apollinare in Classe

covered in 1953 at a depth of about 30 cm below the current floor level. It extended as far as the third pair of columns from the apse and the triumphal arch. The mosaic in the apse was done shortly before the middle of the 6th century, while the decoration of the triumphal arch, subdivided into five horizontal bands according to a typical Byzantine layout, was redone several times over a period from the 6th to the 12th centuries.

The great mosaic decoration of the apse divides into two areas. A grandiose scene of the Transfiguration at the top dominates the decoration. At the centre of a golden sky in which the hand of God emerges from stylised clouds, there is a great jewelled disc containing a cross studded with gems on a background of blue sky dotted with 99 gold and silver stars. At the intersection of the arms of the cross there is a medallion containing the head of a bearded Christ while at the end of the lateral arms are the apocalyptic letters alpha and omega, the first and last letters of the Greek alphabet and symbol of Christ, the beginning and end of all things. Above the vertical arm of the cross there is the Greek word ΙΧθΥΣ which means in Greek "fish" and which can also be considered an acrostic produced from the initials of the Greek words" Jesus/Christ/Son of God/ Saviour". Under the vertical arm there is a Latin inscription which reads: *salus mundi* (Salvation of the world).

The great disc is flanked by the half bust figures of Moses and Elias emerging from the clouds. Underneath three sheep clearly symbolising the apostles Peter, James and John who, together with the two prophets attended the Transfiguration of Christ on Mount Tabor.

The lower part of the apse is dominated by the solemn figure of the patron saint Apollinaris, the founder and first bishop of the Church in Ravenna. He is robed in a white dalmatic and a chasuble dotted with golden bees, an ancient symbol of eloquence, and depicted with his arms outstretched in an attitude of prayer while addressing his prayers to God for the salvation of his followers.

They are represented at his feet in the form of twelve lambs converging towards him on a background of a verdant landscape with rocks, flowers, trees and pines in particular, which are still typical of the coastal landscape of Ravenna today. The landscape features however do not produce any effect of depth as they are arranged on overlapping planes without any natural relationship.

Located in the lower part of the apse between the windows are the first four and most important bishops of Ravenna: Ursicinus, Ursus, Severus and Ecclesius as indicated by the inscriptions located behind their heads. Represented frontally and with a gold crown hanging above their heads and each holding an evangeliary studded with gems, they complete the exaltation of the church and orthodoxy, representing also the historical continuity of the Church of Ravenna founded by St. Apollinaris.

On the sides of the lower part of the apse two large panels, datable to the second half of the 7th century, complete the mosaic programme: on the right a panel containing scenes of sacrifices seems to summarise those depicted in the two walls of the presbytery of San Vitale, since the sacrifices of Abel, Melchisedek and Abraham are represented around an altar. In the left side a panel containing a historical subject, extensively restored in tempera, depicts the bestowal of privileges on the Church of Ravenna by the Byzantine Emperor Constantine IV Pogonatus. In fact it was he, in the presence of his brothers Heraclius and Tiberius and clergymen, who bestowed the privileges, possibly of autocephaly and other tax exemptions, on Reparatus who had been sent by Archbishop Maurus of Ravenna.

The triumphal arch of the apse is complete. At the centre of the top band is a medallion containing a bust of Christ in a benevolent attitude with a bearded face and a severe expression. Depicted at his sides on a dark blue background are the winged and haloed figures of the four evangelists each holding a Gospel (7th century with restorations of the 9th century).

In the band immediately below (7th century), white sheep, symbolising the apostles, are depicted coming out of the towered cities of Jerusalem and Bethlehem and moving in two processions toward Christ. The two cities symbolise the two churches of the Judaic and pagan worlds.

In the third band two stylised palms stand on a blue background (7th century) while at the sides further down the two archangels Michael and Gabriel are depicted like celestial guards on a gold background holding a banner in the right hand bearing the words "Holy, holy, holy", written in Greek. They are wearing magnificent robes typical of court ceremonies comparable with those of Justinian and are the only figures in the triumphal arch ascribable to the original decoration of the Justinian era. Two panels in the bases of the arches depict the busts of the apostles St. Matthew and possibly St. John, the result of a revision at the beginning of the 12th century attributed to artists from Venice.

Justification for inclusion
in the World Heritage List

Sant' Apollinare in Classe has been described as the most impressive example of the Early Christian basilica. In spite of the plundering to which it has been subjected over the centuries, it has conserved all the beauty of the original building: the balanced proportions of the naves, the bright interior bathed in light from the fifty-three windows of the side and central naves plus the five windows of the apse, the elegant succession of arches and the twenty-four marble columns from the east, the simple decoration of the cube-like bases of the columns, the refinement of the dosserets and capitals with acanthus leaf motifs moved by the wind and finally the splendour of the mosaic decoration in the apse in which Byzantine symbolism reaches its apex.

From the iconographic standpoint the apse decoration contains highly original and innovative features: for the first time in the history of Christian art the eponymous saint is represented instead of the Maiestas Domini. This was probably the will of Maximian who had to replace a mosaic containing decorative-symbolic motifs previously planned (which can be inferred from the discovery of a sinopite), with the figure of the first bishop Apollinaris and his most important successors. The purpose of this was to glorify the Church of Ravenna, speaking to the minds and souls of the faithful who came to Classe to venerate the tomb of the martyr, patron and father of the Church in Ravenna.

Through the great scene of the transfiguration (the passage of Christ from human to divine nature in line with the political and religious needs of the Justinian era aimed at reaffirming orthodoxy after the prevalence of Arianism) the orthodox dogma is exalted.

It is not by chance that a great transfiguration scene, with human figures, dominates the apse of the church of Saint Catherine on Mount Sinai, one of the most important bulwarks of orthodoxy, built by Justinian between 548 and 565.

Basilica of Sant'Apollinare in Classe

Unlike this church, and other later churches, the transfiguration of Sant'Apollinare in Classe is represented mostly in symbols becoming "one of the most unusual allegorical representations that art has ever produced".

A story of triumph thus unfolds in the apse, uniting in the glory of God heaven and earth and with the patron saint the entire Church of Ravenna as represented by the four bishops located between the windows. This theme demonstrates clearly the specific desire of Maximian – revealed also in other works – to pay special homage to the saints and bishops of Ravenna and consequently the Church of Ravenna in order to strengthen its authority, something entirely in line with the political and religious policy of the emperor Justinian.

The exaltation of the Church of Ravenna is also expressed in the panel on the left of the apse where, in the second half of the 7th century, a moment of power and glory for the Church of Ravenna was depicted in which special imperial privileges were obtained such as metropolitan autonomy in the context of an old and continuing rivalry with Rome.

The composition of the apse decoration is marked by great symmetry and axial thrust. Extending the arms of the cross the apse is divided into four perfectly symmetrical areas.

Emphasis is given to the division between heaven and earth and therefore the divine and human parts, represented by the first bishop and his successors, by a curved line and the different backgrounds, gold for the first and landscape for the second. The presence of two different expressive languages is due not so much to the presence of two artists with different artistic traditions, but rather to underline different concepts, as in San Vitale.

Essential Bibliography

The bibliography for the historic buildings of Ravenna is vast. The list below contains the main references.

GEROLA, G. (1917), La tecnica dei restauri ai mosaici di Ravenna, in *Atti e Memorie della R. Deputazione di Storia Patria per le Province di Romagna*, Bologna, 4, 2, pp.101-194.

TESTI RASPONI, A. (1929), Annotazioni sulla storia della chiesa di Ravenna dalle origini alla morte di San Gregorio Magno, in *Felix Ravenna*, Ravenna, 33, pp.29-49.

GALASSI, G. (1929), *Roma o Bisanzio. I musaici di Ravenna e le origini dell'arte italiana*, Roma, La libreria dello Stato.

RICCI, C. (1930-37), *Tavole storiche dei mosaici di Ravenna*, Roma, Istituto Poligrafico dello Stato. Libreria.

VON SIMSON, Otto G. (1948), *Sacred Fortress. Byzantine Art and Statecraft in Ravenna*, Chicago, The University of Chicago press.

NORDSTRÖM, C.-O. (1953), *Ravennastudien. Ideengeschichte und ikonographische Untersuchungen über die Mosaiken von Ravenna*, Stockholm, Almqvist & Wiksell.

MAZZOTTI, M. (1954), *La basilica di Sant'Apollinare in Classe*, Città del Vaticano, Pontificio Istituto di Archeologia Cristiana.

DE ANGELIS D'OSSAT, G. (1962), *Studi ravennati. Problemi di architettura paleocristiana*, Ravenna, Edizioni Dante.

SIMONINI, A. (1964), *La Chiesa ravennate. Splendore e tramonto di una metropoli*, Ravenna, Monte di Ravenna.

CORTESI, G. (1966), *Classe e Ravenna paleocristiane*, Ravenna, Longo.

BOVINI, G. (1969), *Edifici di culto d'età paleocristiana nel territorio ravennate di Classe*, Bologna, Patron.

BOVINI, G. (1969), *Edifici di culto di Ravenna d'età preteodoriciana*, Bologna, Patron.

DEICHMANN, F. W. (1969), *Ravenna Hauptstadt des spätantiken Abendlandes. Geschichte und Monumente*, Wiesbaden, F. Steiner.

MONTANARI, G. (1969), Elementi per una ricerca storico-teologica sull'"arianesimo" nella città di Ravenna, in *Atti dei Convegni di Cesena e Ravenna*, Centro studi e ricerche sulla antica provincia ecclesiastica ravennate, Cesena, Badia di Santa Maria del Monte, 1, pp.27-50.

BOVINI, G. (1970), *Edifici di culto d'età teodoriciana e giustinianea a Ravenna*, Bologna, Patron.

DEICHMANN, F. W. (1974), *Ravenna Hauptstadt des spätantiken Abendlandes. Kommentar*, II, 1.Teil, Wiesbaden, F. Steiner.

DEICHMANN, F. W. (1976), *Ravenna Hauptstadt des spätantiken Abendlandes. Kommentar*, II, 2.Teil, Wiesbaden, F. Steiner.

DEICHMANN, F. W. (1989), *Ravenna Hauptstadt des spätantiken Abendlandes. Kommentar*, II, 3.Teil, Stuttgart, F. Steiner.

FARIOLI, R. (1975), *Pavimenti musivi di Ravenna paleocristiana*, Ravenna, Longo.

FARIOLI, R. (1977), *Ravenna romana e bizantina*, Ravenna, Longo.

RIZZARDI, C. (1985), Mosaici Altoadriatici. Il rapporto artistico Venezia-Bisanzio-Ravenna in età medievale, *vol.1 di Biblioteca di Felix Ravenna*, 1, Ravenna, Edizioni del Girasole.

PIERPAOLI, M. (1986), *Storia di Ravenna. Dalle origini all'anno Mille*, Ravenna, Longo.

IANNUCCI, A. M. (1987), Restauri ravennati. Per la fondazione di una storia del restauro musivo, in *Corso di Cultura sull'Arte Ravennate e Bizantina* (Ravenna, 4-11 aprile 1987), Università degli studi di Bologna Istituto di antichità ravennati e bizantine, Ravenna, Longo, 34, pp.179-208.

RIZZARDI, C. (1989), L'Arte dei Goti a Ravenna: motivi ideologici, aspetti iconografici e formali nella decorazione musiva, in *Corso di Cultura sull'Arte Ravennate e Bizantina* (Ravenna, 14-22 aprile 1989), Università degli studi di Bologna Istituto di antichità ravennati e bizantine, Ravenna, Longo, 36, pp.365-388.

IANNUCCI, A. M., FIORI, C., MUSCOLINO, C., (1990) (a cura di), Mosaici a S.Vitale e altri restauri. Il restauro in situ di mosaici parietali, in *Atti del Convegno Nazionale sul restauro in situ di mosaici parietali* (Ravenna 1-3 ottobre 1990), Ravenna, Longo.

RIZZARDI, C. (1991), Paradigmi ideologici ed estetici nei mosaici ravennati di età giustinianea, in *Felix Ravenna*, Ravenna, Università degli studi di Bologna, Centro di studi per le antichità ravennati e bizantine Giuseppe Bovini, 4. s., fasc. 1/2 (135-136), pp.37-62.

CARILE, A. (1991) (a cura di), *Storia di Ravenna. Dall'età bizantina all'età ottoniana*, vol. 2, 1, Venezia, Marsilio.

CARILE, A. (1992) (a cura di), *Storia di Ravenna. Dall'età bizantina all'età ottoniana*, vol. 2, 2, Venezia, Marsilio.

ANGIOLINI MARTINELLI, P. (1992), La cultura artistica a Ravenna, in *Storia di Ravenna. Dall'età bizantina all'età ottoniana*, a cura di A. Carile, Venezia, Marsilio, vol. 2, 2, pp.159-176.

ANDREESCU TREADGOLD, I. (1992) Materiali, iconografia e committenza nel mosaico ravennate, in *Storia di Ravenna. Dall'età bizantina all'età ottoniana*, a cura di A. Carile, Venezia, Marsilio, vol. 2, 2, pp. 189-208.

VASINA, A. (1993) (a cura di), *Storia di Ravenna. Dal Mille alla fine della dinastia polentana*, vol. 2, 3, Venezia, Marsilio.

RIZZARDI, C. (1993), Mosaici parietali esistenti e scomparsi di età placidiana a Ravenna: iconografie imperiali e apocalittiche, in *Atti del 1° Colloquio dell'Associazione per lo studio e la conservazione del mosaico* (Ravenna, 29 aprile - 3 maggio 1993), a cura di Raffaella Farioli Campanati, Ravenna, Edizioni del Girasole, pp.385-407.

IANNUCCI, A. M. (1993), Problemi di restauro e conservazione dei mosaici parietali di Ravenna, in *Atti del 1° Colloquio dell'Associazione per lo studio e la conservazione del mosaico* (Ravenna, 29 aprile - 3 maggio 1993), a cura di Raffaella Farioli Campanati, Ravenna, Edizioni del Girasole, pp. 175-187.

RIZZARDI, C. (1994), L'architettura a Ravenna durante il regno di Galla Placidia: problematiche ed influenze artistiche, in *Ravenna Studi e Ricerche*, Ravenna, Società di studi ravennati, pp. 189-202.

RIZZARDI, C. (1994), L'architettura di epoca teodericiana a Ravenna: aspetti e problematiche, in *Corso di cultura sull'arte ravennate e bizantina. Seminario internazionale sul tema: Ravenna, Costantinopoli, Vicino Oriente* (Ravenna, 12 - 16 settembre 1994), Ravenna, Edizioni del Girasole, 41, pp. 131-148.

RIZZARDI, C. (1996) (a cura di), Il Mausoleo di Galla Placidia a Ravenna, in *Mirabilia Italiae*, 4, Modena, Ed. Panini.

RIZZARDI, C. (1997), I mosaici parietali del XII secolo di Ravenna, Ferrara e San Marco a Venezia: relazioni ideologiche e artistiche, in *"Storia dell'arte marciana: i mosaici" (Atti del Convegno Internazionale di Studi, Venezia 11-14 ottobre 1994)* a cura di R. Polacco, Venezia, Marsilio Editori, pp. 123-134.

RIZZARDI, C. (1997), San Vitale: l'architettura, in *"La Basilica di San Vitale a Ravenna", Mirabilia Italiae, 6, (a cura di P. Martinelli Angiolini)*, Modena, Panini Ed., pp. 21-40.

RIZZARDI, C. (1998), Ravenna, il mosaico nel Duemila: cultura artistica e tecnologia, in *"OCNUS" (Quaderni della Scuola di Specializzazione in Archeologia), 5, (1997)*, Bologna, Ante Quem, pp. 197-206.

RIZZARDI, C. (1998), L'attività edilizia del vescovo Neone a Ravenna, in *"Corsi di Cultura sull'Arte Ravennate e Bizantina", XLIII, (1997)*, Ravenna, Ed. del Girasole, pp. 781-802.

RIZZARDI, C. (1999), L'impianto liturgico nelle chiese ravennati (V-VI secolo), in *"Hortus Artium Medievalium", Journal of the International Center for Late Antiquity and Middle Ages*, Zagreb-Motovun, v.5, pp. 67-85.

RIZZARDI, C. (1999), Il mosaico parietale (V-XI secolo): bagliori di eternità sul mondo terreno, in *"La Forma della luce. Arte del mosaico dall'Antichità al XX secolo" (Catalogo)*, Milano, Electa, pp. 31-35.

RIZZARDI, C. (1999), Le rappresentazioni architettoniche nei mosaici parietali di Ravenna: dal mondo terreno a quello trascendente, in *"Atti del VI Colloquio dell'Associazione Italiana per lo Studio e Conservazione del Mosaico" (Venezia 20-23 gennaio 1999)*, Ravenna, Ed. del Girasole, pp. 637-646.

RIZZARDI, C. (2000), L'arte musiva nell'area alto-adriatica, in *"Adriatico Mare d'Europa. La cultura e la storia"*, a cura di E. Turri, Milano, Cinisello Balsamo, pp. 188-201.

RIZZARDI, C. (2001), La decorazione musiva del Battistero degli Ortodossi e degli Ariani a Ravenna: alcune considerazioni, in *"L'edificio battesimale in Italia. Aspetti e problemi" (Atti dell'VIII Congresso Nazionale di Archeologia Cristiana) (Genova, Sarzana, Albenga, Finale Ligure, Ventimiglia 21-26 settembre 1998)*, Firenze, All'Insegna del Giglio, II, pp. 915-930.

RIZZARDI, C. (2001), Teoderico a Ravenna: il Battistero degli Ariani alla luce dell'ideologia politico-religiosa del tempo, in *"Wentilseo. I Germani sulle sponde del Mare Nostrum", (Atti del Convegno Internazionale di Studi)*, a cura di A. Zironi (Padova, 13-15 ottobre 1999), Padova, Unipress, pp. 101-118.

MONTANARI, G. (2002), *Ravenna: l'iconologia. Saggi di interpretazione culturale e religiosa dei cicli musivi*, Ravenna, Longo.

NOVARA, P. (2003), *"Ad religionis claustrum construendum". Monasteri nel Medioevo ravennate: storia e archeologia*, Ravenna, Fernandel Ed.

RUSSO, E. (2003), *L'architettura di Ravenna paleocristiana*, Venezia, Ist. Veneto di Scienze, Lettere ed Arti.

PENNI IACCO, E. (2004), *La basilica di S.Apollinare Nuovo di Ravenna attraverso i secoli (Studi e Scavi del Dipartimento di Archeologia, n. 8)*, Bologna, Ante Quem.

RIZZARDI, C. (2005), I mosaici parietali di Ravenna da Galla Placidia a Giustiniano, in *"Venezia e Bisanzio. Aspetti della cultura artistica bizantina da Ravenna a Venezia (V-XIV secolo)* (a cura di C. Rizzardi), Venezia, Istituto Veneto di Scienze, Lettere ed Arti, pp. 231-273.

PASQUINI, L. (2005), Il battistero della Cattedrale Cattolica, in *"Venezia e Bisanzio. Aspetti della cultura artistica bizantina da Ravenna a Venezia (V-XIV secolo)* (a cura di C. Rizzardi), Venezia, Istituto Veneto di Scienze, Lettere ed Arti, pp. 327-349.

VERNIA, B. (2005), L'arredo liturgico della basilica di Sant'Apollinare Nuovo a Ravenna, in *"Venezia e Bisanzio. Aspetti della cultura artistica bizantina da Ravenna a Venezia (V-XIV secolo)* (a cura di C. Rizzardi), Venezia, Istituto Veneto di Scienze, Lettere ed Arti, pp. 363-389.

RIZZARDI, C. (2005), Il cielo stellato del Mausoleo di Galla Placidia, in *"Studi in memoria di Patrizia Angiolini Martinelli"*, a cura di S. Pasi, Studi e Scavi del Dipartimento di Archeologia, 10, Bologna, Ante Quem, pp. 277-288.

RIZZARDI, C. (2005), Le immagini vescovili nei mosaici parietali di Ravenna tra V e XII secolo: tipologie, significati, considerazioni, in *"Atti del IX Colloque Internaz. AIEMA"*, Roma, Ecole Française de Rome, pp. 1189-1202.

RAVENNA. DA CAPITALE IMPERIALE A CAPITALE ESARCALE (2005), Atti del XVII Congresso Internazionale di Studi sull'Alto Medioevo, Ravenna 6-12 giugno 2004), Spoleto.

AUGENTI, A. - BERTELLI, C. (2006) (a cura di), *Santi Banchieri Re. Ravenna e Classe nel VI secolo. San Severo il tempio ritrovato* (Ravenna, 4 marzo - 8 ottobre 2006), Milano, Skira.

RIZZARDI, C. (2006), Ravenna fra Roma e Costantinopoli: l'architettura del V e VI secolo alla luce dell'ideologia politico-religiosa del tempo, in *"Acta Congressus Internationalis XIV Archaeologiae Christianae"* a cura di R. Harreither, Ph. Pergola, R. Pillinger, A. Pulz (Vindobonae,19.-26.9.1999), Città del Vaticano, Pontificio Istituto di Archeologia Cristiana, I.vol, pp. 671-680.

AUGENTI, A. - BERTELLI, C. (2007) (a cura di), Ravenna tra Oriente e Occidente: storia e archeologia, *(I Quaderni di Flaminia, n.8)*, Ravenna, Longo.

AUGENTI, A. - BERTELLI, C. (2007) (a cura di), *Felix Ravenna. La croce, la spada, la vela: l'alto Adriatico fra V e VI secolo*, Milano, Skira.

RIZZARDI, C. - VERNIA, B. (2007), Scene circensi nei mosaici pavimentali provenienti dal Palazzo di Teoderico a Ravenna: ipotesi ricostruttive e significati, in *"AISCOM. Atti del XII Colloquio dell'Associazione Italiana per lo Studio e la Conservazione del Mosaico"* (Padova-Brescia 14-17 febbraio 2006), Tivoli Scripta Manent Ed., pp.119-130.

SPADONI C., KNIFFITZ, L. (2007) (a cura di), S. Michele in Africisco e l'età giustinianea a Ravenna (Atti del Convegno *"La diaspora dell'arcangelo San Michele in Africisco e l'età giustinianea"*. Giornate di Studio in memoria di Giuseppe Bovini, Ravenna, 21-22 aprile 2005), Milano, Silvana Editoriale.

RIZZARDI C. (2007), I mosaici parietali di Ravenna di età giustinianea e la coeva pittura occidentale e orientale, in *"S. Michele in Africisco e l'età giustinianea a Ravenna"* (Atti del Convegno *"La diaspora dell'arcangelo San Michele in Africisco e l'età giustinianea"*. Giornate di Studio in memoria di Giuseppe Bovini, a cura di C. Spadoni e L. Kniffitz, Ravenna, 21-22 aprile 2005), Milano, Silvana Editoriale, pp. 83-97.

FARIOLI CAMPANATI, R. (2007), I mosaici pavimentali di Ravenna e di area adriatica in età giustinianea. Il tappeto musivo di San Michele in Africisco, in *"S. Michele in Africisco e l'età giustinianea a Ravenna"* (Atti del Convegno *"La diaspora dell'arcangelo San Michele in Africisco e l'età giustinianea"*.Giornate di Studio in memoria di Giuseppe Bovini, a cura di C. Spadoni e L. Kniffitz, Ravenna, 21-22 aprile 2005), Milano, Silvana Editoriale, pp. 179-191.

RIZZARDI, C. (2007), Chiesa e Impero nel Medioevo: le Abbazie di Ravenna e dell'area padano-adriatica fra tradizione innovazione, in *"Hortus Artium Medievalium", vol.13, 1*, Zagreb-Motovun, pp. 117-136.

RIZZARDI, C. (2007), Le sale di rappresentanza dell'Episcopio di Ravenna nell'ambito dell'edilizia religiosa occidentale ed orientale dal tardoantico all'alto medioevo, in *"L'Audience Rituels et cadres spatiaux dans l'Antiquité et le haut Moyen Age"*, a cura di J. P. Caillet et M. Sot, Ed. Picard, Paris, pp. 221-239.

RIZZARDI, C. (2007), Fasi e aspetti della Cristianizzazione attraverso le immagini musive: l'esempio di Ravenna, in *"La Cristianizzazione in Italia fra Tardoantico e Altomedioevo"* (IX Congresso Nazionale di Archeologia Cristiana, Agrigento, 20-25 novembre 2004), a cura di R. M. Bonacasa Carra, E. Vitale, Carlo Saladino Editore, Palermo, vol.I, pp. 797-822.

MOSAICORAVENNA.IT (2007) (a cura del Centro Internazionale di Documentazione sul Mosaico), Mar, Cidm, Ravenna.

PASQUINI, L. (2008), *Iconografie dantesche. Dalla luce del mosaico all'immagine profetica*, Longo Ed., Ravenna.

Ten years later

More than ten years have now passed since the inscription of Ravenna in the World Heritage List of Unesco. Formal approval was given on 7 December 1996 at the 20th session of the World Heritage Commission at Merida in Mexico. On 14 March 1997 Bernd von Droste, director of the World Heritage Centre, gave Ravenna the parchment reproduced at the beginning of this publication. The original is kept in the Municipal Residence.

The parchment states, in accordance with the Convention for the Protection of Cultural and Natural Heritage, that "inscription in the list validates the exceptional universal value of a cultural or natural asset in order to ensure its protection for the benefit of the entire world". Ravenna has been inscribed on the basis of no less than four of the criteria envisaged for cultural heritage. This means that, according to Unesco, our monuments represent a masterpiece of human creativity; they reveal interrelations of important values, with reference to the development of architecture and art in buildings, they provide exceptional evidence of a cultural tradition, they are an exceptional example of buildings and architectural features that illustrate an important phase in the history of mankind.

Correspondence to the criteria of Unesco, which was stated in the substantial work of drafting the application, is made available again in this publication at a distance of ten years: appearing here for the first time in the English and Italian languages are the sections of the document which, as requested by Unesco, give the historical background, description and justification for inclusion in the World Heritage List.

The decision to present the candidature of Ravenna was taken in 1994 by Pier Paolo D'attore, the first Mayor of Ravenna elected directly by the citizens thanks to the new law of 1993. Candidature was a prime objective for the Municipality which, together with the owners of the monuments, the Superintendency for Environmental and Architectural Heritage1 and the Archdiocese of Ravenna, coordinated the work for presenting the necessary documentation. In addition to the Municipality, the Superintendency and the diocese, the University of Bologna also participated with the valuable contribution of Professor Clementina Rizzardi of the Faculty of Humanities and Philosophy and author of the text; the same University that set up its Faculty of Conservation of cultural Assets in Ravenna in 1996.

The Municipality as not involved directly in the management of the monuments destined to become World Heritage but acted as spokesman regarding the desire for acknowledgement of the identity and exceptional value of the city, thus stating a journey of cultural valorisation which has characterised recent years and which continues today with great intensity.

1 Now Superintendency for Architectural Heritage and Landscape

14 March 1997: Bernd von Droste, Director of the World Heritage Centre, presents the Vice Mayor of Ravenna Donatella Zanotti the parchment reproduced at the beginning of this publication, in the presence of the Vice President of the Cabinet and the Minister of Cultural Assets Walter Veltroni.

The process of candidature, started in the spring of 1994 was long and involved many people. The Mayor Pier Paolo D'Attore, who unfortunately passed away a few months after inscription in the List, entrusted the coordination of the work to the then Councillor for Culture Filippo Brandolini. For the Superintendency for Environmental and Architectural Heritage, Anna Maria Iannucci then Superintendent and the architect Emilio Agostinelli monitored carefully all the phases in drafting the dossier. The Archdiocese of Ravenna, with the then Archbishop Monsignor Luigi Amaducci and the "Opera di Religione" provided indispensable cooperation and a new and most valuable photography project. Drafting of the original text in English was assigned to Manuela Farneti with later revisions and additions for this publication by Scuola Interpreti. The texts relating to the monuments were provided by Clementina Rizzardi of the Faculty of Humanities and Philosophy of Bologna University.

The definitive document in English was presented to Unesco through the Ministry of Foreign Affairs in February 1995. This volume contains only the descriptive sections of the candidature presented in due course: the dossier sent to Rome and Paris consisted of other documentary and technical material not shown here. Unesco assigned the investigation to ICOMOS (International Council of Monuments and sites) which after a visit to Ravenna in

December 1996 expressed its favourable opinion of inscription in the List which was announced in Mexico in December 1996 and in Ravenna in march 1997.

In the years following the work has been continued jointly in a spirit of cooperation. To give just a few examples: the same cooperation experienced in presentation of the candidature was repeated successfully on occasion of obtaining the finances necessary for the Jubilee in 2000. The same collaborative effort distinguished the drafting of the management plan for the Unesco Site thanks to an institutional agreement signed by the Municipality, the Regional Administration for Cultural and Landscape Heritage of Emilia-Romagna, the Superintendency for Architectural Heritage and Landscape of the province of Ravenna and the Archdiocese of Ravenna-Cervia in February 2005. This agreement identified the Municipality of Ravenna as the body responsible for drafting the Management Plan of the Unesco Site because it is responsible also for the development and promotion policies of the territory. The Management Plan was presented in May of the same year and its updates are now part of a customary cooperative effort.

Ten years after inscription in the List, what changes have occurred? The monuments with their millennial history have certainly not: their protection and conservation is amply ensured by those responsible who, even this year, have continued to work towards this end. For this reason the texts by Clementina Rizzardi (although the author comments that the texts are not up to date with the most recent studies) which we have published in celebration of one decade since inscription in order to disseminate increasingly the knowledge and awareness of the exceptional value of the heritage that Ravenna has been called to keep. What has changed is that the city has acknowledged, primarily to itself, its identity as a city of culture, a producer of cultural events, its destination as a place of cultural tourism, as a city that innovates and applies new ideas also in the organisation of culture through old and new relations of cooperation and agreement. Finally, it is a city that, projecting itself into the future, continues to enquire into its own past and history in order to give back knowledge and awareness to the citizens, visitors and, as Unesco reminds us, to future generations.

Maria Grazia Marini
Director of the Unesco Site Management Plan
The Early Christian Monuments of Ravenna

Published by the Municipality of Ravenna

Fabrizio Matteucci, Mayor
Alberto Cassani, Councillor for Culture
Maria Grazia Marini, director of the Tourism and Cultural Activities Service

Monsignor Giuseppe Verucchi, Archbishop of Ravenna
Monsignor Guido Marchetti, Director of the "Opera di Religione" of the Diocese of Ravenna

Carla Di Francesco, Regional director for Cultural Heritage and Landscape of Emilia-Romagna
Giorgio Cozzolino, Superintendent for Architectural Heritage and Landscape of the provinces of Ravenna, Ferrara, Forlì-Cesena and Rimini.

The owner of the monuments of Ravenna inscribed in the World Heritage List of Unesco is the Archdiocese of Ravenna-Cervia (Galla Placidia, Neonian Baptistery, St. Andrew's Chapel, Sant'Apollinare Nuovo and San Vitale) and the Italian State (Arian Baptistery, Theodoric's Mausoleum, Sant'Apollinare in Classe). The diocesan monuments are managed by the "Opere di Religione" organisation, the state owned monuments are managed by the Department of the Superintendent of Architectural Heritage and Landscape of the provinces of Ravenna, Ferrara, Forlì-Cesena and Rimini and the Regional Administration.

Text by Clementina Rizzardi

Graphic Design: Tuttifrutti, Ravenna

Photos
Municipal Archives Ravenna: 20, 23, 24, 28, 30, 32, 44, 46, 50, 59, 61, 62, 64, 66, 68, 70, 74, 77
Tomaso Baldini: 26, 40
Massimo Carioti: 37, 51, 53
Gianluca Liverani: 22, 45, 48, 49, 72, 75
Maurizio Montanari: 16, 25
Bruno Pini: 84
Nicola Strocchi: 17, 19, 31, 39, 43, 55, 65, 67, 69, 71, 73, 78, 80, 85, 94-95
Luigi Tazzari: 2, 4, 6, 8, 10, 12, 29, 33, 34, 35, 42, 56, 81, 83
Fabrizio Zani: 91

Vitaliana Pantini, of the Tourism and Cultural Activities Service, collaborated in the selection of the photos.

Printed by Filograf Litografia S.r.l. Forlì

January 2009